Creative Urban Youth Ministry

A Resource for Youth Workers

Glandion Carney

**Foreword by
Charles Colson**

STANDARD PUBLISHING
Cincinnati, Ohio   18-03168

The material in Chapters 9 and 10 and the Resources section was contributed by Gayla Cooper Congdon, Executive Director and Co-Founder of AMOR MINISTRIES, a nondenominational mission organization based in San Diego, California.

Unless otherwise indicated, Scripture quotations are from the HOLY BIBLE: NEW INTERNATIONAL VERSION, Copyright © 1973, 1978, 1984 International Bible Society. Used by permission of Zondervan Bible Publishers.

Library of Congress Cataloging-in-Publication Data
Carney, Glandion
    Creative urban youth ministry : a resource for youth workers / Glandion Carney ; foreword by Charles Colson
      p.   cm.
    Includes bibliographical references.
    ISBN 0-87403-798-0
    1. Church work with teenagers. 2. City churches. I. Title.
BV4447.C367   1991
259'.23'091732--dc20

                        90-48481
                        CIP

to my closest friends, Gene and Gloria,
for their commitment to young people
and their deep love for God

Foreword

GLANDION CARNEY IS one of those marvelously gifted young men being used by God today to breathe fresh life into His church and to call Christians to a renewed commitment to help meet society's most urgent needs. The call could not be more timely.

For if the church is to function as the body of believers God intended us to be, we cannot do so as cloistered congregations gathering in our own protected enclaves. We must come together as one people, the holy nation the apostle Peter wrote about. And we must work together to make God's invisible kingdom visible in every dimension of life—particularly those areas the church has long ignored.

That's why this book on ministry to urban youth is so exciting. In Prison Fellowship's ministry, I deal with many young men and women in prison who have not come to know Christ in a personal way because they have not seen the church as the vital, living body God intended it to be. Tragically, far too often they have seen instead hypocrisy, exclusivism, and retreat to the high ground of the "safe" suburbs. They've also often seen the inner-city church virtually abandoned, starved for resources and unable to offer help. So, feeling that Christians have rejected them, they have rejected Christianity.

These young people need to know that the church of Jesus Christ cares; they also need role models who will walk with them, challenge them, disciple them. They need Christians who will live with them on their turf, instead of passively waiting for kids to come to them on their terms.

The inner-city gang often takes the place of the fellowship of the church in these young people's lives. This book offers practical advice on how concerned Christians can be "interpreters" of the gospel, offering youth the only real alternative—the love, power, and dignity of life in Christ.

If enough Christians heed Glandion's challenge, Prison Fellowship's work in the prisons could be cut back dramatically. Many urban young people would be diverted early from criminal involvement to be won and trained instead as disciples in the kingdom of God.

I also heartily commend Glandion's work because of his focus on the Word of God. Far too many Christians today—in their zeal to do good—are forgetting that the whole foundation of our work rests upon the absolute primacy of the Word. Glandion understands that our call is one of faithfulness to the Word and obedience to Christ. And like all leaders, starting with the greatest Teacher of all, Glandion instills in others that same truth. "You and those you disciple should be trained to hear in the Word of God a call to action," Glandion writes. "Through our practical obedience, we express to God and others our love of Christ and our gratitude for His grace."

As Glandion applies his insight and energies to such a vision for urban youth, I hope he will serve as a powerful stimulus to the evangelical church as well. The inner cities are filled with people who will never cross the threshold of our churches; our task is to take the church to them. Glandion has provided us with a grand challenge to bring the suburban church into partnership with the inner city church, and for us to live up to all God has called us to do—and to do so together as one body. In the process we will make His invisible kingdom visible in the places of greatest need.

—Charles Colson
Chairman of the Board
Prison Fellowship

Contents

Commendation

IF YOU ARE a pastor or Christian youth worker who has a heart for the salvation of inner-city youth, this book is for you. As a pastor, this book has helped me keep in focus the fact that the church is in a battle against the forces of evil that threaten the very existence of one of our nation's most valuable resources—urban youth. Glandion reveals some of the struggles our youth have to face as they grow up in tough inner-city environments that are infested with gangs, drugs, crime, illiteracy, broken families, unemployment, lack of self-esteem, and hopelessness.

Although these facts are disheartening, the book is not all gloom and doom. Glandion inspires us with hope as he reveals a systematic approach to redirecting the lives of our youth culture through the institution of an urban youth ministry. The book challenges us to resist the all-too-common temptation of procrastinating in the area of youth ministry. We must direct our ministry to them at a very early age—before other influences have time to make a major impression on them. However, we, as church leaders, are first called to become good Christian role models for our youth by exhibiting commitment to God, the family, and the church.

Dr. James E. Martin
Senior Pastor
Mt. Olivet Baptist Church
Portland, Oregon

Chapter One

Youth Work:
The Biblical Basis

WILLIE BROWN HAD it made. At least he thought he did. Talented and creative Willie was a 16-year-old I knew growing up in Oakland, California. My friends and I thought he was bound for a career in football, but too soon he found he was headed for something far different.

Willie desired only two things in life—to drive a big car and get "loaded." One day, doing both, he plowed into a truck on Railroad Avenue. Willie died a young man. He had wasted the precious few years given him by God.

You might say, "That's an isolated incident." Unfortunately, it's not. This kind of thing is all too common. After I finished speaking at a Chicago rally several years ago, a 17-year-old approached me to say, "I don't have time for God. I don't have room for Christ in my life." Then he walked out of the auditorium and got in a waiting car. In minutes he, like Willie, was dead, obliterated in a tragic accident.

Listen to the writer of Ecclesiastes:

Remember your Creator
    in the days of your youth,
before the days of trouble come
    and the years approach when you will say,
    "I find no pleasure in them."
Ecclesiastes 12:1

Neither Willie nor that young man at the rally remembered the Lord in their youth. As a result, they led wasted lives, died senseless deaths, and faced the judgment of God without coming to know Him.

That sounds rough, doesn't it? Well, it's the hard truth, and we will never change those sad facts unless we first admit them. You—the one who works with and loves young people in the urban church—can help to save young people like these from similar tragic ends.

Through the grace of God, you can help draw young people to the Lord and help instill godly values in them. The alternative is losing your teens to the powerful forces of an unfeeling society, one that may destroy them. You are the representative of a caring, personal God who wants each of your teens to take advantage of their God-given potential.

God Cares About Young People

In the commendable interest of finding out what the Bible says about the poor, the dispossessed, minorities, women, the aged, we have perhaps overlooked its great emphasis on the molding of young lives. The Bible is packed with promises for young people and for the ones who work with them. In God's Word we find the illustration of the church as God's garden plot. We need to see that children are not simply seeds waiting to take root, but are lively flowers that blossom and need pruning.

Again and again in the Scriptures we see God using adults to tend His garden, to nurture these plants in need of care.

This is where you come in. God has a special plan for you in His care of these, His valued young people. Consider the role that parental examples played in the lives of three young men: Shadrach, Meshach, and Abednego. Nebuchadnezzar ordered them thrown into a furnace when they refused to worship an idol of the earthly king (Daniel 3). Unlike others similarly threatened with death, these three young men would not bow to ungodly pressure. They acted on the values previously taught them by elders, and God blessed them for it.

Think also of Joseph. Sold into slavery as a teenager by his own brothers (Genesis 37), this outcast eventually became the prime minister of Egypt. Because of the trust and knowledge of God that his father, Jacob, had undoubtedly helped to give him, Joseph was able to resist some strong temptations. He refused to become involved sexually with Potiphar's wife, or to become bitter over the years in prison, or to seek revenge against his brothers when they came to him in desperation for food. Living what his parents and his God had taught him, Joseph became a testimony to the loving faithfulness of the Lord.

David was called to the service of God at an even younger age than Joseph (1 Samuel 16). Even before what we might call his full maturity, David served the Lord in the court of King Saul, on the battlefield against Goliath and the Philistines, and in the fields, tending his sheep and writing psalms of praise to his Lord. David's life shows clearly that God did work specifically and seriously with young lives. He still does.

The New Testament also provides us examples of God's concern for youth. The apostle Paul served as a father to Timothy, teaching and training him by example, and Timothy became a church leader. Other young people Paul helped may remind you of teens you know. For example, John Mark was a missionary dropout and Onesimus a runaway slave. Paul saw something of worth in these young men and took the time to forgive them, teach them, and help them on their way to maturity.

What do all these young people have in common? They possess qualities just like yours and the youth to whom you minister—faults and strengths, the ability to fail and succeed, the capacity to feel despair and joy. In a word, they each had humanity. None of them had mysterious, superhuman traits. They had what your teens have, the simple ability to serve God.

And something else—they had help from their friends. You can be a friend to your teens. You, the youth worker, are one friend who can demonstrate the care of God for inner-city youth. Through God you can recognize their true value as children of God. You, with the church, can help to build caring structures around them, and help them appreciate and use the Bible as a way to change, deepen, and expand their values. You do this by teaching and modeling the truth, focusing on the practical application of the Bible rather than theological understanding.

Then, their ability to serve God may be transformed into their desire to follow Him.

You Care About Young People

The Bible does more than recount past successes adults have had training young people; it provides specific guidance. In Proverbs, God, through Solomon, offers young people two different images of how they might order their lives. The prostitute (Proverbs 5—7) offers all promise and no fulfillment. The pleasures she offers are like the morning fog; they will soon burn away. Like the world, with its superficial and dangerous values, the prostitute promises life and joy—but delivers death and destruction. Wisdom (Proverbs 1, 3, and 8), however, gives all that God wishes us to have. For the one who follows her, wisdom unfolds a life of trust, discipline, and true love. The image of the prostitute shows that bad choices and negative values have a certain glamour and appeal, but also have negative consequences. Wisdom, on the other hand, sets the standard for right choices. The youth worker must be a stable influence in the life of the young person, helping him make right value choices.

Solomon urges young people to pursue wisdom. Calling on youth to heed the word of their parents (Proverbs 1:8), Solomon tells them to

> Lay hold of my words with all your heart;
>   keep my commands and you will live.
> Get wisdom, get understanding . . .
>   *Proverbs 4:4, 5*

To know wisdom is in reality to know God and to know how He would have us live. And in the Bible, when you know something, you not only believe it, you act on it.

Perhaps it would help you to think of yourself as a modern Solomon urging the teens you know to follow wisdom. Like the young people of Solomon's day, your teens also know the strong draw of the world. It beckons and whispers, seeking to entrap the young person in the pursuit of pleasure. You know from experience and observation that the world will never deliver what it has promised. But the young person probably doesn't know it, and as a result, you find yourself locked in battle with Satan on his turf. He would have your young people believe that the brief but empty enjoyment of the world is the best available; you want them to see the rich promise of a life of commitment, service, and achievement.

As you begin your work, remember that God considers every teenager to be a person of worth. The message that they matter to God and others is one not often heard in the world where they live. At school, on the streets, and on the playground, they face terrible pressure to conform. If your teens fail as athletes, dress differently, or act "religious," they are likely to experience the scorn and ridicule of the crowd. The Bible tells teens that they are of value to God, but the group claims that they have worth only if and when they go along with the gang. Feeling rejection, your teens may do things that violate God's standards and rob them of their individuality.

Perhaps it is at this low point that you walk into their lives. The teens in your church or your community are feeling the heavy pressures of home, school, and the gang. Here you come with this thing called the gospel. Do you preach at them, hand out tracts, and tell them that God loves them?

No. Well, if that's the wrong way to do it, then what's the right way?

Look to the Bible for an answer to that question. Jesus didn't glide to earth like some superhero. He came into a dirty stable in an out-of-the-way town. He struggled and agonized; He knew temptation and suffering firsthand; He came as God in the flesh. We call this coming of God into human life the "incarnation." This is what God would have you become for those young people He loves so much—an incarnation of the love of God. You tell them what God would have them know, that they matter a great deal to you and to Him. And to do this you don't have to pretend that you're some kind of superhero. After all, you're flesh and blood just like the young people you're trying to reach. Like them and like Jesus, you know temptation and suffering, and God hardly expects you to claim that you don't. Because you don't have to pretend, you're free to tell and to show teens the one thing you know for certain: God has an unending, unlimited love for them.

As an "incarnation" of the love of God, you must also remember that these teens need to understand the gospel on their own terms. It is their world you must enter, their language you must speak, and their needs and problems you must address with your love and the wisdom of God's Word.

Young People Are Part of Christ's Body

In addition to God's love for each individual, the Bible speaks repeatedly of the fact that every person who knows Jesus is a gifted member of His body. The young person is not only an individual loved by God, but he is also an invaluable part of that body. No part of the body can say to the whole, "I don't need you," nor can the whole body say that to any part (1 Corinthians 12).

Many of the young people you deal with have little or no real sense of family, and many of them no doubt feel they can't belong to a group because they have no special talents. You, as a minister of Christ's body, have the difficult but joyous task of showing them that Christ and His body on earth, the church, need each one of them, no matter what their circumstances or their shortcomings. Never forget that fact: young people need the church, and the church needs them.

Teens need to be taught the truth about themselves because they have not grown up understanding their true value. They often come from a low self-esteem base and need to learn self-esteem, self-knowledge (their true gifts and abilities), self-love, and the ability to share their true selves in society. They need the constant affirmation that the church can offer them, by placing them in a context where they can be affirmed, developed, and strengthened as valuable members of God's family.

Teenagers think about their need for God more than most adults realize. The home and church should be places where youth learn about Him. If they aren't, false cults and religions will rush in to fill the vacuum. For urban youth, these false gods may take the form of success and pleasure. Ideally, parents should help youth put the pull between materialism and Christianity into perspective. But sadly, many times this doesn't happen in the home environment.

When teenagers need encouragement from people other than parents, they should be able to turn to the local church for support. Since the days of Jesus, churches have been a great source of hope, and there is no reason for it not to be so today. After all, the first churches were made up of Christians who gathered together to celebrate and preach the message that Jesus has been raised from the dead. The message that no power, not even death, has ultimate hold on Jesus and those who love Him is still the true message of the church. If you can tell young people that message in their own language and show them how they can live out that message in their own environment, then you will be continuing the work parents have begun. If parents have not done the work, you can begin it through the power of the gospel and your example of love.

Several people from a church led me to Christ when I was a teenager. They spent time with me, let me ask questions, and permitted me to fail. When they saw something good in me, they told me about it and gave me praise, and when I needed to be challenged, they challenged me. Because of their example, I feel I need to make special, personal impact on young people. What I need to do, in other words, is to continue to make disciples in the same way those men made a disciple of me.

John Perkins of the Voice of Calvary Ministries in Mississippi, has done just that. Years ago he went to work in the community of Mendenhall. He strove to help Christian young people see their potential and their responsibility. One of the young people he discipled was Dolphus Weary, who has now taken leadership over that work in Mendenhall and has an important position on the Voice of Calvary staff. The process of discipling goes on. That's reassuring!

Go As Jesus Did

As a youth worker, you can have no better friend than the Bible. In the Bible you will find that God has a definite interest in youth and that He has a call for people like you to bring young people to the Lord and to disciple them in His ways. Time after time the Scriptures tell of young people whose lives have been changed by their spiritual elders. And just as you find in the Bible examples of leadership, you also find principles for leadership. You will discover in the Bible that God wants the same things for all people, young and old. He wants young people to claim His name and acknowledge Him as Lord; He wants adolescents to think well of themselves, to have what we might call a positive self-image; He wants young people active in the life of their church; He wants them to serve as disciples, and in doing so to make new disciples; and His will is for teenagers to grow in the faith into and throughout adulthood.

Of you, the one who works with these young people, God wants the willingness to love, forgive, and endure.

He knows how hard it can be to live and lead the Christian life. But just as He communicated His judgment and love best by walking among men and women, you can best make His love known through your concern, compassion, and patience.

LIFE RESPONSE

1. The tug between wisdom and adultery as described in the Book of Proverbs is a daily reality for urban youth. Illustrate this with the following reading and mime. Choose two good readers and have them alternate verses, Reader 1 beginning with Proverbs 1:8 and Reader 2 with Proverbs 1:22.

If your group is dramatically inclined, divide it in half and have some mime the words of Reader 1 and the others the words of Reader 2. Reader 1 ends with verse 19 and Reader 2 with verse 33. After these parts are played, have the group read in unison verses 20 and 21.

2. Discuss with your group how "Wisdom calls aloud in the street" (Proverbs 1:20). List on a chalkboard or a tablet on an easel the negatives that youth have experienced as a result of self-destructive behavior. List the positives they have experienced when they have followed the ways of wisdom. How can youth encourage each other on the way toward wisdom? List their answers.

3. Have group members write a statement on the subject, "How the Bible relates to my life." Discuss their answers as you share insights gained from this chapter.

Chapter Two

Somebody's Child

"MEANINGLESS! MEANINGLESS!"
  says the Teacher.
"Utterly meaningless!
Everything is meaningless."
Ecclesiastes 1:2

This thought is daily reality for many young people. It is especially true for many urban youth. For them, life can appear as bleak and hopeless as the author of Ecclesiastes portrays it at the beginning of his book.

One response is mentioned in Isaiah and quoted by the apostle Paul:

"Let us eat and drink,
  for tomorrow we die."
1 Corinthians 15:32

If all life has to offer is despair, then let's eat, drink, and be merry. If nothing but what we see around us is real, and what we see is poverty and powerlessness, we owe it to ourselves to have as much fun today as we possibly can. There is no tomorrow.

But that is a big *if.* If, Paul said, Christ was not raised from the dead, then those who believe in Him will not rise either. They are without hope. But *if He did rise, if He does live,* then there is a tomorrow, there is hope.

It is a false kind of security, a cruel deception, to believe in the death of tomorrow. Still, this is the only faith many urban youth have. They have no power and no hope. Without these, they do what the Bible says they are bound to do—live it up today, die tomorrow. It's the only kind of security they think is available.

Your mission is to free them from this slave-master death through the power and hope of the gospel of Jesus Christ. But before you do that, you've got to know—if you don't already—what it means to be a slave to sin and death, to be a young person trapped in the prison of urban life. You've got to be aware of the problems these young people face. They live in a world where positive values are constantly challenged. And because they often simply don't feel good about themselves, they become slaves to a value system that destroys their creativity, and sometimes, their lives.

The Problem of Negative Self-Image

Do you want to know what it means to have no hope, no power? Just imagine what it would be like if you could not read or write. It is hard for you to get or keep a job. But even if you do have a job, you are limited in your ability to communicate with those you work with. You have difficulty conveying what you feel, and the reasons for your feelings, to those you love because you cannot use words well. Without the ability to read and speak well you cannot really control your future.

There are other reasons urban teens feel hopeless, but this is the situation for many urban youth. If the gospel message is going to sink in and grab your young people, you need to know how and why these strong, deadly forces have such hold on them. You have an ability, and with it a power, that many of the young people you are trying to reach have never known and may never know.

Many urban children, from the beginning of their lives, exist in a world where few people are good models of discipline and self-control. You have the chance, and are indeed called, to create a positive model for them. Unfortunately, too many of these young people are born into families where there is no history of success, only one of shame and failure. These young people have parents, grandparents, and great-grandparents who had all been told by their society that because they were poor white, black, or hispanic, they were nothing, could do nothing, and should expect nothing in life. Of course, your message to them is that they are worth something. You may be living proof that God can create something out of nothing, even today, as He created on that first day.

Urban young people come into a world where too many of the people around them have said, in effect, "You're nobody going nowhere." Because of this, people who ought to be serving as examples of success and hope for youngsters offer only the example of failure and fear.

Somebody Going Somewhere

If urban teens are going to grow, they need to be nourished by seeing that others like themselves have solid values and peace and joy. Without positive role models to emulate, they are left trapped in an environment where each day everyone and everything seem to say: "You're a nobody who's going nowhere." When all that they see seems to feed them negative ideas, urban youth have little power to improve their lot in life. And there is no basis for hope that things will change.

As you reach out to these young people, to show them love and care and to provide them with good examples to follow, you may face another problem. Because so many of them have had no models of authority to look up to, they may distrust you at first. Chances are that anyone who has been in authority over them has either failed or oppressed them. You have to realize that you're trying to overcome not only their negative feelings about themselves, but you're also going to have to show them that you are not trying to take advantage of them in some way. They must see that you deserve their trust.

For many young people in America, education offers a way out of hopelessness. In school they learn a skill or a trade, and with it they get a job. At least that's the way it's supposed to work. For many urban youth, it doesn't work that way at all. They learn one set of skills to survive at home and on the street and another set of skills at school. They often don't see the connection between education and life. Most of them simply don't see how a better life can be built with educational tools. All too often, young people in the city don't see that what's offered to them in school is what they'll need to survive and prosper in the larger world. And when they do discover that they need those tools, it's almost always too late for them to get them.

Since they received little or no help in developing good discipline and self-control at an early age, and because they have failed to pick up the necessary education, many urban youth, by the time they're teenagers, have no record of achievement to which they can point with pride. Too often, their past is nothing but a fuzzy record of failure. It's hard to have hope for the future if there's nothing in your past to make you believe in yourself. For most urban youngsters, the past seems like nothing more than a ruin and rubble of wasted time and lost opportunities.

The Gang

This rule about the city youth's past has one unfortunate exception. Many of these young people have worked for and given themselves to one thing—the gang. Poor youngsters in the city are like youngsters or adults anywhere else. They crave acceptance from participation in something larger than themselves. God made us for each other, never intending us to remain alone. But in the city, the gang offers the kind of friendship and fellowship often found nowhere else.

In a sense, gangs are like churches for many of these young people. Both the gang and the church make them conform to certain beliefs and ways of behaving, and in return affirm young people and build self-esteem by offering protection and a feeling of belonging. The difference between the church and the gang is in the results of living its value system.

A gang constantly affirms the values that bond them together in relationship. The sense of family or fraternity supplies the motivation for membership for the person with low self-esteem. The teen member believes the gang needs him—he is likely to have an assigned task in the gang related to his gifts. The gang helps its members to feel they are persons of worth and potential, creating an image of power and prestige through the use of their language (special code words often give teens a feeling of acceptance), and by inflating their importance and asserting superiority over other gangs. When you're feeling worthless, a gang activity gives a feeling of worth. The gang comes to have a place of importance and value in the life of the teen.

The gang usually has a clear code of ethics:

1. Weakness is not tolerated.
2. The gang comes before the family.
3. Gang members value each other.
4. Gang members do not act outside the gang rules.

Therefore, to meet the needs of teen gang members, a good discipleship group will need:

1. A clear code of ethics.

2. An understanding that the young people are persons of worth and dignity.

3. The ability to communicate to them that they are persons of worth and dignity.

4. The commitment to work with weaknesses and give skills (in communication, work, education) that will build their confidence, and to instill in each young person a clear set of values.

Society has often devalued these urban young people, which has pushed them to seek the affirmation of the gang. When you reach out to one of these youngsters, you're competing with the claims and promises of the gang. By the time you meet him—let's say when he is 12 or 13—there's a good chance that he has already given three, four, or more years to a gang. Having put a lot into the gang, a young person will tend to hold on very hard to it and its values.

As you try to draw teens away from the immorality, drugs, or violence involved with a gang, you have to realize that you may be taking them away from the only true family they have known. You're trying to displace the only environment where these teens have been shown they can do anything or be anything important. You can provide them an alternative by building within your church a true community of love, support, and acceptance. Your goal is to make sure that in God's family, youth find as much a sense of acceptance as they had found in the Devil's gang.

A World of Illusions

The apostle Paul said that if Christ was not raised, we are without hope. Because they have no hope for the future, it is hard for urban youth to live at peace and with meaning in the present. A world without hope is a world of death.

Think for a minute about the images presented to youth on TV, on the street, and in magazines and newspapers. Each day, these youngsters are bombarded by signals that tell them that it is indeed best to "eat and drink, for tomorrow we die." If you drive into any city, you'll see that almost every billboard proclaims the glories of alcohol, sex, or the "good life." For many in American society, the pursuit of selfish pleasure has come to be the only source of meaning. When you're having a good time—or at least what everyone tells you is supposed to be a good time—you can forget, even if only for a few hours, how bad things really are.

We all know too well the sorry facts about how hard it is to get and keep a job if, for example, you're young, black, and poorly trained. Urban youth have few chances. Every day they see those images of supposed success and happiness. But the pressures under which they live often prevent attainment of these images.

As a result, city youngsters will often turn to the few areas where success does seem possible. Sports heroes, television and movie personalities, music stars—these are all people who have made it. They have broken out of the prison of the ghetto. They seem to have escaped from the clutches of despair that strangle so many young people in the city. They have grown up with a past of failure and ruin, but they have somehow used their talents to create hope for themselves.

The problem with this worship of the exceptional hero—the video personality, the NBA all-star center, the young comedian—is the fact they are just that—exceptions. By definition, there can be very few exceptional people in life, very few poor people who can become rich through their athletic or musical talents. For most of us, the road to happiness is paved with much harder and less glamorous kinds of work.

The hard realities of life for city youth mean that even limited success seems in the hands of a system that doesn't care. Shut out from either the glamorous or the tough ways of "makin' it" in their world, many young people turn to drugs and crime for a way out. What most people on the outside can see very clearly, urban youth can't see until it is too late; they can't see that drugs and crime are no way out of poverty and frustration. Instead, the quick fix can only lead them deeper into the very hopelessness they're trying desperately to get away from.

Summary:
Characteristics of Urban Youth

Through God's Word and because of His grace, urban youth can be drawn to the Lord and reach their God-given potential. Their basic needs are as follows:

1. Physical
   a. Food, clothing, shelter
   b. Parental supervision and protection
2. Emotional
   a. Love and security
   b. Praise and encouragement
   c. Responsibility and achievement

3. Social
   a. Self-acceptance
   b. Acceptance from others
   c. New experiences
4. Intellectual
   a. Development
   b. Expression
   c. Stimulation
5. Spiritual
   a. Morality
   b. Proper values
   c. Personal relationship with Jesus Christ
   d. Ability to express their faith

Usually an urban youth belongs to an extended family. Several households, related through friendship, children, or marriage, may join together under one roof in order to survive. There are few fathers in the home. The mother is often the family leader who is responsible for the discipline and nurture of the young people. Even though the mother may be the only adult role model in this home, her influence may be inconsistent because she has to work outside the home to support the family. This often leaves the oldest child in charge of the other children in the home, and it also leaves him with the responsibility for himself. This provides the opportunity for the young person to look to the streets for influence.

Many unmarried urban teenage girls are pregnant. Some view it as a status symbol. To the young girl who wants something of her own or someone who loves and depends on her, it can seem to provide a sense of security.

Irregular meals and a steady diet of junk food negatively affect their health, moods, abilities, energy, and relationships. Lack of material needs can hinder their sense of security and well-being. Because of overcrowding

in the home, the young person has no real place to call
his own. Due to limited resources and the lack of medical
insurance, minor illnesses go untreated and major illness
places a tremendous financial burden on the family.

Urban schools are overcrowded, with a high student/
teacher ratio. Facilities are often inadequate. Violence is
a frequent occurrence at school, and more of the teacher's
energy goes into maintaining control than into teaching.
Parents support education to a point—they want their
children to attend school, and yet the parents don't
attend conferences or activities to support the school. As
a result, the young person becomes indifferent. Education
mostly occurs by watching television or by exposure to
street life. Without a strong education, the young person
has a hard time developing the ability to verbally articulate her feelings, thoughts, or ideas. Instead, the young
person expresses herself through her behavior, positive or
negative.

By the time the urban young person has reached ado-
lescence, he will have been the victim of a violent crime
or the witness to a violent crime in the home, neighborhood, or school. The young person may be the victim of
emotional or physical abuse. He may be encouraged to be
violent at home.

Other experiences may be:
1. Sexual activity
    a. Receives inadequate instruction about sex and
        its abuses
    b. May be sexually abused
    c. Sees many unwed pregnancies
2. Drug and alcohol abuse
    a. Personal involvement—parents may be the
        provider
    b. Family involvement

3. Instability
    a. Moves frequently because of eviction
    b. Is transferred from one relative to another
    c. Has few personal possessions
    d. Lacks a daily routine
    e. Lacks consistent attention and discipline
    f. Instability of environment results in low self-esteem and insecurity
4. Religious orientation
    a. Is drawn to the occult
    b. Has many misconceptions about the church—sees it as a place with a lot of rules
5. Fear and frustration
    a. Experiences prejudice and discrimination at an early age
    b. Often unemployed; sees little chance to be successful and productive
    c. Lacks motivation in accomplishing goals because of an absence of ordered environment
    d. Little positive affirmation causes him to expect to fail
    e. Experiences feelings of inferiority in school because middle-class values are the standard by which they are educated
6. Early assumption of adult roles
    a. May not have experienced a childhood
    b. Survives on the streets
7. Strong group feelings
    a. Peer pressure can lead to gang involvement
    b. Strong family loyalty

Urban youth seem to have no hope, so they live for today and today's pleasures. Effective urban ministry can change that. Through the local church, it can create an environment in which young people develop a sense of security, a sense of belonging. The church can be a place where the attitude of unconditional love is lived out. Young people can learn to love unconditionally. They can find a sense of freedom from the need to earn love on the streets, where love comes at a price (sometimes the price of their lives).

The church can also affirm their gifts and teach them how to be responsible with those gifts. Maybe for the first time in their lives, they will be given the opportunity to think for themselves and express their ideas and thoughts.

We have a generation of young people who are drifting away from the moral fiber many families were founded on. Judges 2:8-15 speaks about a generation of people that grew up not knowing God or the things He did for Israel. Our urban youth today don't know the Bible or its relevance to the struggles they face in day-to-day life.

The Power of the Risen Lord

This chapter may have seemed gloomy to you, and the job before you may have seemed too hard. But remember, Jesus never ignored the hard truth about things. He did hate and still hates the power of death. He wept before the grave of Lazarus and actually sweat blood as He waited for His own crucifixion. But in the end, He went through death, and in going through it He made it possible for us to have hope.

Let these words, written by the apostle Paul, comfort you.

> But this precious treasure—this light and power that now shine within us—is held in a perishable container, that is, in our weak bodies.

Everyone can see that the glorious power within must be from God and is not our own.

We are pressed on every side by troubles, but not crushed and broken. We are perplexed because we don't know why things happen as they do, but we don't give up and quit. We are hunted down, but God never abandons us. We get knocked down, but we get up again and keep going. These bodies of ours are constantly facing death just as Jesus did; so it is clear to all that it is only the living Christ within (who keeps us safe).

Yes, we live under constant danger to our lives because we serve the Lord, but this gives us constant opportunities to show forth the power of Jesus Christ within our dying bodies.

2 Corinthians 4:7-11, The Living Bible

The stage is set. With the Lord's help, you can be an important player.

LIFE RESPONSE

1. A major problem for urban youth is negative self-image. A big part of your job is helping them overcome this. Think and talk positively. Hang a mirror in your meeting place. Use a grease pencil to write this slogan on the glass: "I'm Somebody." Each time a member of the group walks by, she will see a different reflection than the one the street offers.

2. The gang is key for many urban young people. A big part of what it offers, the church can offer—acceptance, friendship, and fellowship. Discuss with your

group the dynamics of gang support. Have them describe for you how it works. Then ask for their suggestions as to how the church could support youth in as meaningful but more positive ways. Implement the best ideas in a real commitment to providing your youth with an alternative to the gang.

3. This exercise should get your group interacting with God's perspective of the lure between material possessions and the spiritual life. It's hard for urban youth not to feel bitter about going without what the billboards and TV proclaim as the good life.

Read the parable of the rich fool in Luke 12:13-21. Talk about the parable with your group, especially Jesus' teaching in verses 22-34. Then divide the group into units of at least five young people each. Have them make up words to match a commercial ditty of their choice to illustrate what Jesus is saying. The title of their lyrics could be "You Can't Take It With You." Have each group of performers sing their creation to the others.

Chapter Three

Christ's Child

GOD IS OUR refuge and strength,
    an ever present help in trouble.
Therefore we will not fear,
    though the earth give way
    and the mountains fall into the heart of the sea.
                              Psalm 46:1, 2

As we begin to look at the role of the church in the lives of urban young people, a good place to start is with these verses from Psalm 46. At first, they may seem far removed from the church as we know it and as God has made it. What, we might ask, does all this talk about the God of the Old Testament have to do with the ghetto kid from New York City's Bronx, Los Angeles's Watts, or Chicago's Cabrini Green?

Quite a bit, I think. Before the time of Christ, God dwelt in a special way with His people, the nation Israel. When the psalmist called God "an ever present help in trouble," he was saying something profound about God's strength and love. No matter what life-shattering events went on in their world, Israel could know that their God's intent for them was good. They need not fear, though the mountains slip into the sea.

The Church as Source of Strength

Today, God's people are a body that knows no geographic, ethnic, or economic boundaries. The New Testament repeatedly refers to the church as Christ's body on the earth. Like the Jews, whose God was their powerful loving refuge, today's Christians should also be able to think of the church—Christ's body—as a source of strength and shelter.

At this point, you may be wanting to say, "That's not what I'd call my church. Instead of being the shelter from life's storms, it seems to create them; instead of serving as a source of help in times of trouble, it seems to be the source of trouble." But notice that I didn't say that every church always has been, is, or will be that strong shelter. Such is simply what God wants it to be, what He calls us to make it. In this chapter, I'll try to point out ways your work can help to make it a better strength and shelter for young Christians.

When we go to God and His church for shelter, we do so because we know the destructive power of the storms that threaten us. The church is and must continue to be a place where young people find real help in dealing with the difficult problems involved in things like drugs, sex outside of marriage, crime, poverty, and fear.

But you can't deal with a problem that you ignore or pretend does not exist. Jesus hated death, and in His own way, He feared it. But He didn't ignore it; He overcame death by confronting it and going through it. In a similar way, the church can never become a place where the evils of drugs, improper sex, and the like, are conquered until it becomes the place where they are confronted.

When Jesus talked about the church to His disciple Peter, He didn't say, "Well, Peter, you'll have to protect my church, keep it hidden and safe from all the evil things that might hurt it." Instead, He said with utmost confidence, "You are Peter, and on this rock I will build my church, and the gates of Hades will not overcome it" (Matthew 16:18). Paul, who suffered greatly for Christ, met his hardships head-on with faith. "For I am convinced," he wrote to Roman Christians in the first century, "that neither death nor life, neither angels nor demons, neither the present nor the future, nor any powers, neither height nor depth, nor anything else in all creation, will be able to separate us from the love of God that is in Christ Jesus our Lord" (Romans 8:38, 39).

Perhaps we, as twentieth-century Christians, can better understand what the church means by dwelling for a moment on the earliest Christian church. That original church, we read in the Gospels and in Acts, was made up of men and women who had been depressed and discouraged. Their master and teacher Jesus had suffered a senseless and shameful death. Downhearted, they had already begun to scatter when word spread that Jesus had been raised to new life by God.

The earliest churches were places where the followers of Jesus gathered to give thanks and worship God for the resurrection of Jesus. In that resurrection, they saw the justice and love of God. Through the risen Jesus, God offered the forgiveness of sins and the promise of eternal life. Those first Christians were literally brought together by the news of grace and power in Jesus Christ. Without the news, they would have gone their separate ways, in shame and despair.

Our primary desire in coming to church should be to

give thanks to God for His salvation. When we come to church, we are like a person who has just had a cast put on a broken bone. We know that the healing process has begun, but is far from complete. We are thankful for the healing already underway, and we have come to a place and people, the church, where we know such healing will continue as we experience the forgiveness of God and the love of our fellow Christians.

Christina is one such person. She is a 15-year-old girl who was taken away from her family by the state because of abuse. After two months of living in a shelter and coming to a local Bible club for teens, she has accepted Jesus Christ as her Savior and Lord. "Now I know there is Someone who really loves me, and that I'm not a bad girl like my parents tell me I am," she said. "That's why they say I'm here, but I know it's not true." Christina is now sharing the love of Jesus with other girls living at the shelter.

Jimmy has lived in the Cabrini Green section of Chicago for all of his fourteen years. He is one of six children raised by his mother; his father is absent. Before he met a youth worker from LaSalle Street Church, he was influenced by local gangs and was in and out of school. He felt swallowed up by the intensity of wanting to be a man, and he lived out this intensity by trying to see how many children he could father by age 18. But then the youth worker began to share with Jimmy the message of Christian love—going with Jimmy to camp, visiting him weekly at his home, enrolling him in a literacy program. Because that youth worker cared, Jimmy came to the Lord Jesus. He still struggles with the influences of his environment—the lack of a father, the influence of gangs —but his involvement in the church is helping him with his personal and spiritual development.

Kim is another. She is a high-school sophomore who

hasn't come to Bible club much because she is fighting cancer. She has to wear a wig because of chemotherapy, and this makes her feel insecure in public. But after hearing the gospel, she accepted the Lord and is now being discipled by a student leader. Her cancer may continue, but the healing of her life has begun.

In the long history of many groups that have experienced poverty and powerlessness, the church has been the only place where needy and broken people have been able to find help and healing. We weaken that powerful potential of the church when we live according to what has been, in many ways, the official "gospel" of American life, the gospel of individualism. People who believe that they can conquer all their troubles on their own will neither take from nor give to the church as much as the less fortunate have taken and given.

When I look back on one of my own experiences, I think I know why Jesus called the poor in spirit "blessed." Several years ago, my wife became seriously ill, and I called my pastor to ask that some of the leaders of our church come to pray with her. He came that night, at midnight! The next day, a group of elders came to pray. The day after that, several people from the church brought meals for my family. In that process of giving and receiving, I saw the grace of God at work in His church.

Youth Worker as Interpreter

The young people you will be bringing into the church know little, if anything, about Jesus. A large number of them come from homes and streets and schools where so little is known or taught about Jesus that you'd have a hard time knowing He had ever lived. To many of them, the gospel and the guidelines of the

Christian life are as foreign as they were to the people who lived in first-century Palestine, Corinth, or Rome. That is one of the first and most important things for you to remember as you work to bring young people into the life of the church.

If, let's say, they come to you from a gang, the language and rituals of the church will sound as strange to them as the lingo and code words of the street may sound to you. In some ways you are a translator, helping youth to understand the sermons they hear and the Bible and other books they read. Before your interpretation, these things may sound like a foreign language to young people.

In the first chapter, I spoke of the need for you to become "an incarnation of the love of God" to young people. That sounds vague, no doubt, but here we have a good chance to see specifically what it means in the life of young people in the church. When we say Jesus became incarnate, we mean that He took on human flesh, that He came to us to reveal God to us where we are. You can do this for urban young people by bringing the truths of the gospel, the message of a sermon, or the contents of a book to them in their own language. It may seem a simple or obvious task, but it is an absolutely essential one if you are to draw the young person fully into your fellowship.

By bringing a young person into the fellowship of the church, you are in reality bringing her under the lordship of Christ. Think of yourself as helping to extend, in some small way, the kingdom of Christ on earth and in time. Your part in this work of the kingdom has a lot to do with helping these young people to acquire new values, a new purpose.

"If anyone is in Christ, he is a new creation," Paul writes in 2 Corinthians 5:17. "The old has gone, the new has come!" According to Jesus and Paul, the church is supposed to be the place in which we can see clear evidence of the growth of that new order. But what is the distinctiveness of that new order? What makes the church something different from every other institution or group the young person may know? Paul lists the aspects of the fruit of the Spirit as "love, joy, peace, patience, kindness, goodness, faithfulness, gentleness and self-control" (Galatians 5:22, 23).

Perhaps you are thinking, "What does all this talk about love and peace and joy—good things, by the way, things we all believe in—have to do with values? We want to know what to tell the kids is right and what is wrong; we need lists of dos and don'ts, not lists of general qualities, no matter how nice sounding they are." But positive values can have a powerful effect.

The Power of Positive Values

We, as creatures, tend to dwell on the negative aspects of just about anything. For some reason, we think that if we just put a label of "evil" on certain practices and can then avoid doing those things, we will have satisfied God with our goodness.

Jesus, however, was not satisfied with such a simplistic approach to the Christian life. Shortly before His death, He was approached by a Pharisee—a Jewish religious leader who lived by an incredible code of dos and don'ts—asked, "Which is the greatest commandment in the Law?" People perhaps expected Jesus to say, "Worship on the Sabbath." Or, "Don't commit adultery." Or, "Don't drink or go to wild parties." Instead, He said, simply and to the point, "Love the Lord your God with all your heart and with all your soul and with all your mind.' This is the first and greatest commandment. And the second is like it: 'Love your neighbor as yourself.' All the Law and the Prophets hang on these two commandments" (Matthew 22:37-40). Jesus emphasized the positive in His summary. There is much value in our doing so as well.

I think there is a second reason why we shouldn't think of values as largely a matter of dos and don'ts. It may sound odd, but the church can help to keep young people from "doing the don'ts"—such as drugs, premarital sex, and crime—by stressing the positive aspects of the Christian life. If we as individuals and as a church show that we love God with all our heart, soul, and mind, and our neighbors as ourselves, we'll be much more likely to aid the young person in developing Christlike values.

Think of it this way. We've called the church God's family. We all know from our own experience that we naturally respect and obey parents who are loving, patient, and compassionate to each other and us, more than we respect and obey parents who are angry, jealous, and selfish. If we hope to build values into the young person in the church, we have to take care to sink a deep and firm foundation of love and concern.

The Power of Purpose and Promise

But we should seek to give young people something more than a set of positive values. In all probability your teens have suffered, have known what it means to be put down, cut off, and shut out. Paul would say such injustice is the "stuff" of the old order and should have no place in the church of the new order. God's church should be a place in which "hatred, discord, jealousy, fits of rage, selfish ambitions, dissensions, factions and envy" (Galatians 5:20, 21) have no place, for those very things have made the world such a tough and unfair place in which to live.

Ideally, the church should give young people a sense of purpose in life. That is why it is so important for you to bring teens as fully as possible into the life of the larger body. If your young people truly feel they belong, that they have an identity in the church, they won't have to fight and claw their way to an identity on the streets or in school. Since Christ died for them, and the church reinforces their place in His body, young people can find worth and purpose there. The church can actually put back the identity the urban world has stripped away.

You can also specifically help teens develop a sense of purpose by showing them that someone cares enough to expect some things from them. God has commanded us to minister to broken people in body and spirit, and to preach and live the gospel. Get those young people to make a hospital visit with you or take a trip with them to the home of an elderly shut-in. If you can get young people to acknowledge and fulfill their responsibilities to God and other Christians, you will have gone a long way toward helping them to develop a sense of purpose.

Since urban youth most frequently come to church from an environment in which they have experienced real suffering and injustice, you must strive to make the promise of the gospel as down-to-earth and lively as possible. Sure, the gospel offers us all the promise of eternal life with Christ, but if we limit its promise and power to the distant heavenly future, we may fail to keep many of the very young people drawn to Christ in the first place.

"We are free to do anything," the Corinthians told Paul, but he said in return, "Everything is permissible'—but not everything is constructive. Nobody should seek his own good, but the good of others" (1 Corinthians 10:23, 24). That principle should guide us as we seek to understand the church and the place it has in the experience of urban young people. "Your attitude should be the same as that of Christ Jesus," Paul tells us.

> Who, being in very nature God,
>   did not consider equality with God something to
>   be grasped,
>   but made himself nothing,
>   taking the very nature of a servant.
>   *Philippians 2:5-7*

You need to view the church as God's body on earth, in which He has ordained worship of himself and fellowship among His followers. In the next chapter, I am going to talk about some of the specifics of discipleship, but in this chapter I hope I have shown you the powerful promise of the church and the need for you to bring the young person as fully as possible into the life of the church.

LIFE RESPONSE

1. On a chalkboard or a tablet on an easel, write out Psalm 46:1, 2. Read it aloud, slowly and with feeling. Then ask your teens what pictures the words bring to their minds.

On a large piece of butcher paper, or better yet, a wall of your meeting room, have your group outline and then paint what they see in their minds. Have someone write the words of the Psalm as a title. This exercise should reinforce for your young people that God is their source of strength.

2. Enlist your group's help in comparing the language of the street to the language of the church. Block

off two columns on a chalkboard or a tablet on an easel. Head the first column, "Street Talk." Have the group members name some jargon while you list it. This should go quickly.

Then, head the second column, "God Talk." As a group, brainstorm words, phrases, or ideas that provide the Christian parallels to the positive images evoked by street talk or the Christian alternatives to the negative aspects of the street. This exercise should get everybody involved interpreting the faith for today.

3. As a means of reinforcing the power of positive values, lead your young people in a discussion of Jesus' response to the question, "Teacher, which is the greatest commandment in the Law?" (Matthew 22:36).

Explore with them the implications of Jesus' answer. Ask them how they might live out the greatest commandment at home, in school, in church.

Chapter Four

Growing Up in Christ

THIS MAY BE the most important chapter of the book because it deals with what I see to be the highest priority of the church: spiritual growth in its members. The prompting and care of that growth is the most crucial business of the church, and this applies to young people as much as it does to adults.

The most important goal for a youth worker is *to build into the young person an appreciation and love of God.* Your goal must be to make God more than just a word young people use to make themselves happy. Young people need to incorporate God into the many choices they make in everything from daily personal life to choice of career. You want to make the following words come alive in the people you are discipling.

> Trust in the Lord with all your heart
> and lean not on your own understanding;
> in all your ways acknowledge him,
> and he will make your paths straight.
> *Proverbs 3:5, 6*

Think of yourself as a planter of signposts pointing to the values and concepts that will serve as guides for young people throughout life.

The Beginning of Spiritual Growth

As a teenager, I desperately wanted to grow as a Christian, but in my own way. I did, for example, read the Bible regularly. Anxious to learn, when I didn't understand something I'd go to my youth worker and ask for an explanation. I soon found, however, that it was one thing to read the Bible and quite another matter to make its words apply to my life. For example, I felt very spiritual when reading the Bible, but not while washing dishes. I could feel "good" reading the Bible or playing ball, but not while I was doing a job I didn't want to do.

My struggle as a young Christian was probably like the experience of teens in your church; perhaps like your own struggle. I'm sure you know what I mean. We end up playing ball rather than mowing; we do the dishes but with great resentment, and then we feel like guilty failures because we haven't lived in obedience to God in the ordinary routines of our lives. We keep making the same mistakes, yielding to the same temptations, repeating the same sins.

But this is where spiritual growth really counts. Spirituality is a practical discipline, not some elusive, mystical experience. Christian teens can learn nothing more important than how to integrate their spirituality into daily living. But before this can happen, they must, with your help, learn about the grace of God through personal experience.

Spiritual growth begins with spiritual birth. That may seem obvious, but I feel I have to say it because youth workers often assume that all of the young people with whom they are working are believers, only to discover, to their surprise, that many are not. Some of the people in your group many be living double lives, going through the motions, saying the right words, and even fitting in nicely with the group. Many may be acting one way toward their parents and church and another way toward their peers. What they may be missing is the personal reality of trust in Christ as Savior and Lord.

I like to compare salvation to owning a fancy car. Imagine a beautiful new Firebird with a deep burgundy color and camel's hair upholstery. You are all excited and call your girlfriend to go for a drive. You get yourself together with your hair combed and your best clothes on. But when you hop in the car and put the key in the ignition, you hear nothing but a click. Only then do you discover that the car has no engine! Picture yourself pushing that beautiful car down the street and you've got a good image of what it's like to try to live the Christian life without the Spirit of God in us.

Before a young person can become a Christian, he must admit a need for God. The sinner lives separated from God, and in Romans 3, Paul says that all of us begin our lives in such a condition. But Christ died on the cross to take the penalty for our sinful rebellion, and He arose from the dead to give new life to us who are sinners. We can only explain the radical change that occurs in Christians by calling it what it is, the grace of God. Ephesians 2:5-7 says that because God loved us, He "made us alive" and put us into a relationship of union with Christ.

This new life is like a seed planted in the heart. As growth begins, a plant appears and begins to bear fruit. The fruit of the Spirit—with love, joy, peace, and patience (Galatians 5:22, 23)—can grow only when the Christian life is watered and nourished by the Spirit of God. God wants this fruit to appear in the lives of His people, because He wishes all of us who claim His name to be conformed to the image of His Son, Jesus. Ephesians 2 calls the Christian God's handiwork, undergoing reconstruction as a spiritual dwelling for God. How does this reconstruction go on? It proceeds when the individual walks in the pattern of good works (discipleship) prepared by God for every believer. Your job is to help young people understand and experience what Ephesians 2 is talking about.

The Growth Process

Before I can lead a person to Christ, I must establish a friendship with that person. I need to know what she is like, how she thinks, and what she feels. Often we preach at people and never become personal. For them to see Christ in me, they've got to know me—and for me to show Christ to them, I've got to earn the right to be heard.

The strategies for teen evangelism are many, including taking teens to large-group evangelistic events, going after strategic teens (those with influence in the group that others will follow), and getting the gospel to all the diverse subgroups within your youth group (gang members, athletes, well-adjusted young people, and so on). But the one essential aspect of evangelism common to all teens is person-centered contact. You operate in their world, not your own; you speak to their needs; you begin at their starting point. Don't try, for example, to change their outward appearance to suit your desires. Paul's gospel stayed constant, but his approach changed with each person he met. A teenager once asked, "If I don't accept Jesus, will you still be my friend?" That's a very perceptive question. Person-centeredness keeps on caring even after rejection.

Our goal is to present the gospel to our teen friends in a straightforward and sincere manner. We must keep on guard against substitutes for presenting the gospel. Having exciting activities and a good rapport with the teens are both good things, but they are inadequate if done alone. Also inadequate are spiritual generalities —the old, "God is great, God is good" speech. We do believe in God, and Jesus is a good friend, but we have to get more specific than that.

Finally we have to keep in mind the long-range goals of evangelism for our entire ministry. We must be patient with those we're ministering with, stand by them until they're ready for Christ, and follow through with our care as they grow in Him, until they in turn are able to bring others to Christ and disciple them (2 Timothy 2:2). This is the fruit of our labor, the fruit that will remain.

Resting in Christ

Why, then, do so many young Christians fail to bear fruit? Why do they shrivel up, having allowed their spiritual life to be choked off by cults, false teachers, or the pursuit of materialism?

We don't emphasize the lordship of Christ. It's easy to talk about accepting Jesus, because everyone can do that. Jesus was a "cool dude," we say, and wouldn't it be nice to have Him in your life? "He's free," we say. "Take Him. He doesn't cost a thing." That's not the whole story. Yes, salvation is a free gift, but discipleship, or growth in the Spirit, costs and demands a great deal. A disciple accepts the authority and obeys the commands of the one he follows. Many young Christians are not prepared to endure and triumph in such a struggle, because many of us in teen evangelism have pointed out the benefits but not the responsibilities.

When all that has been said, however, we have to come back to the fact that while the Christian life involves a good deal of struggle, its foundation is a state of rest or relaxation. Before we can grow spiritually, we must be at rest in Christ. Jesus made the offer: "Come to me, all you who are weary and burdened, and I will give you rest" (Matthew 11:28). A group of Protestant Christians has answered the question, "What is the chief end [goal or duty] of man?" this way: "To glorify God and *enjoy* Him forever." I like to think of resting in God as coming in from the cold world with its numbing hassles to warm up by the fire of God's love. Our enjoyment of God refreshes and revitalizes the soul and recreates the power of the Spirit in us.

The Value of Small Triumphs

We can say that spiritual growth begins when we focus in on Jesus Christ and fellowship with Him, but what does this restful fellowship mean in practical terms for you and the youth with whom you are working? I think we rest in God primarily when we worship and when we pray. Worship takes place when the members of the church gather on Sunday to praise the Lord together. But worship is also portable—it's an attitude and activity you can carry with you wherever you go and whatever you do. You can give thanks to God and see His goodness in such simple things as a juicy hamburger, a new coat, or a chance to visit a close friend in another city. Christian young people must learn to worship God by giving Him thanks for all the little things that give them pleasure and joy.

Prayer also includes giving thanks to God, as well as seeking guidance and help for our needs and the needs of others. Prayer is the intercom that connects us to God. As a teen, I thought of prayer in a different, and I might say, dangerous way. I had a Cecil B. DeMille conception of God. Up on some mountain He was going to make a miraculous appearance with thunder and lightning and a great voice coming down from above. I wanted a special, personal message from God. I now realize, as an adult, that I can get just that—a special message from God— through His Word and in my thoughts. It's not necessarily a mysterious process, this way that God works through our minds as well as our emotions. We can count on His guidance as we put Him first in our plans through following the Scriptures.

The writing of this book provides an example of what I mean. Over the years I have met many youth workers who have been looking for help. As I discerned a genuine need, a desire grew in me to communicate the things God had taught me. I prayed about this book and reflected on the challenge it would present. All the time, I was guided by the certainty that if the project was of the Lord, it would come to fruition, and that if it was not of the Lord, the book would never appear. God honors our thoughts and concerns and works through them to help us grow; we don't have to wait for some special revelation. Faced with problems and challenges each day, we need to reflect on them, commit them to the Lord in prayer, and apply the insights and principles we have learned.

I remember facing an English exam in high school. Not having studied, I turned to my Cecil B. DeMille God in prayer to ask Him to give me the answers I needed. After all, He knew the correct answers. But unfortunately He wouldn't let me in on them, and I flunked. Feeling that God had let me down, I didn't realize until later that I had a wrong image of God. The God of the Bible hadn't let me down, but the strange "Santa Claus in the sky" I worshiped had failed to come through. By letting me fail, the true Lord God had shown me a better way of living a responsible Christian life. Needless to say, I studied for my next English test! Every young person needs to learn, as I did, how prayer fits into daily practical life.

To grow spiritually also means to grow in wisdom, which I think of as the knowledge of life in the way God intended it and the ability to live that kind of life. According to Proverbs, wisdom begins with the fear of the Lord (Proverbs 9:10), the recognition of the greatness and sovereignty of God. Young people who have this attitude will be open to those teachings that lead to wise behavior and actions based on true knowledge.

"How can a young man keep his way pure?" the psalmist asks, and then he answers his own question—"By living according to your word" (Psalm 119:9). That's one very important way to develop maturity in the young people you are trying to disciple. You'll want to make sure that that seed of Scripture sinks into the rich soil of the young person's life and takes root. It's very easy for us to admire and all but worship that "perfect" teen who quotes Scripture easily, speaks eloquently, and does all the "spiritual" things. We can gaze in admiration at the flashy flower without checking on the depth of its roots and the amount of nourishment it receives. Quick and impressive appearances are hardly as important as slow, but steadily developing realities.

Several years ago the *Sanford and Son* television program had a "religious" character, Aunt Esther, who dressed in old-fashioned clothes and repeatedly said, "Thank You, Jesus." She refused to have anything to do with cynical characters like Fred Sanford. "Get away from me—I'm sanctified!" was her motto. She wore her spirituality like a badge to frighten those around her and keep them from getting too close. You might say of her that she was so heavenly she was of no earthly good.

Instead of escaping from the world, Christian young people should be taught to see how God's grace touches all the ordinary events of life. Spiritual growth should —no, must—relate to the nitty-gritty areas—family relationships, dating, school, television, and sports—or else the Christian faith will mean little to the young person in a practical sense. Growth involves a daily struggle, because even though we are all new creatures in Christ, we still have a lot of the "old Adam" in us and will be tempted each day as a result.

But young people can't fight the battle and win if they remain alone. Once when I was ministering in Cook County jail, a Christian inmate told me of the struggle he was having with cussing. God simply didn't seem to be answering his prayers for deliverance from this bad habit. I suggested that instead of asking God to take away his cussing, he should pray Paul's prayer in Ephesians 1:17, "I keep asking that the God of our Lord Jesus Christ, the glorious Father, may give you the Spirit of wisdom and revelation, so that you may know him better." And to know Him better is to reflect on what He has done and is doing in our lives, to know He is there with and for us.

Being With and For Young People

If you reflect on what Christ has done for you, you will reflect for young people the love and certainty of Christ. You should be a walking mirror in which those whom you are discipling can see the image of Christ. To reflect Christ you don't need to put on a spiritual act to try to hide your own humanity. Be honest and transparent, confessing your failures and weaknesses. Then, witness to the power of God's grace in your life. Be a model of practical Christian living by doing what I call "natural hanging out," going shopping, attending a ball game, or taking in a movie with your young people to show them how Christianity gets down to their level.

You can also help these young people develop spiritually by monitoring their progress and looking for ways to help them experience some kind of success. Talk to them about the patience they need to overcome the temptation to fight with a brother or sister; help them develop the courage and security to avoid the pressures of gangs and groups; model for them love toward a person in need.

In all of this, look not for final victory but for triumphs in small battles. Help them deal with the real problems they are facing, rather than the ones you might imagine them to be facing. You can do this by working with them to set reasonable goals, to be able, for example, to say no when the friends at school invite them to smoke in the bathroom. That may seem insignificant to you, but to the teen the ability to win that kind of battle, to overcome that kind of temptation, is all-important. If Christ can't be the Lord over such small areas of life, how can He possibly be Lord over the much larger areas?

In all of this, never lose sight of the fact that God has called you to be a stable center of gravity for these young people in a very unstable world. Keep bringing them back to the principles of God's Word. It's fine to let them express their feelings about parents, school, and God, but always make sure to point them back to God's Word and to their responsibility to live according to that Word. It's easy for a youth worker who wants to be accepted to become wishy-washy at this point. Believe it or not, though, most young people want to be confronted with the truth so that they can then build their lives around it.

In short, all of the means by which Christians grow —worship, prayer, Bible reading, and daily obedience— need to be part of your youth program. Be sure to work on them yourselves, but also do them with your young people—not just for them, but with them!

LIFE RESPONSE

1. Growth in Christ is hard to measure, and it's full of ups and downs. Suggest to your teens that they keep a growth journal as a record of their relationship with the Lord. There are various ways you can approach journal keeping; one is to write love letters to God in response to His presence in your life. If you suggest this, be sure to keep a journal yourself, and show it to your young people.

Weekly or monthly, look back together on the ups and downs you see reflected in the pages. Each individual in your group must have the right to decide how much, or how little, to share with the others. Journal keeping can be a vital record of spiritual growth, but some will be more comfortable sharing from it than others.

2. Get your teens' reaction to the following statement, "A human being's chief goal in life is to glorify God and enjoy Him forever." Repeat the statement one or two times, and see what they think. Try to cite Scripture in support of this thought (you could start with Matthew 22:37 and Psalm 100).

3. During the next week, keep a record of how much time you spend with your young people. Imagine that "natural hanging out" is a job assignment, and your employer wants to evaluate your time log. Concentrate on spending more time than you usually do with your teens doing everyday things. At the end of the week, evaluate the results.

Chapter Five

Success in Christ

WHAT DOES IT mean to survive? And, what does it take to succeed? The suburban, middle-class youth likely thinks of survival in psychological terms—"Can I make it in the competitive worlds of school and business? Can I stand the pressures of dating and marriage?"

To the urban young person, on the other hand, the word "survival" will probably signify something much closer to the literal meaning of the word—"Can I get a skill or job that will help to put the food on the table? Can I avoid the tempting pressures of drugs and violence?"

In this chapter I want to offer some specific advice as to how you can help urban youth in their struggle to survive and succeed. In many ways, I'm writing this chapter to balance the scales on the matter of discipleship. For too long they've been tipped almost totally on the side of heavenly spirituality, and as a result, we've treated the earthly side of discipleship far too lightly. Some youth programs do concentrate on practical training and the building of skills, but the church has largely ignored the development of skills for survival and success as an aspect of discipleship.

Jesus himself set the standard for this kind of discipleship when He sent His disciples out with this warning, "I am sending you out like sheep among wolves. Therefore be as shrewd as snakes and as innocent as doves" (Matthew 10:16). To put it in contemporary terms, Jesus was saying, "Have street savvy. Know what's 'going down' so that you can avoid trouble as you follow me." Jesus Christ needs committed men and women like you to help people meet the tough challenges of urban life. He needs people like you, who will walk with teens as Jesus walked with needy people in first-century Palestine.

Survival of the Fittest

Charles Darwin, the nineteenth-century English naturalist, coined the phrase "survival of the fittest" to describe the process by which animals have supposedly evolved over the years. You don't have to believe in evolution to see the appropriateness of that phrase for life in the city. Jesus isn't pleased with that reality of the city. For example, it's interesting to notice that the Book of Revelation pictures the home of the redeemed as one large city where people fellowship forever without suffering pain and death. In your own way, by helping Christian young people to survive and succeed, you are helping to make the kind of people who can change the city of suffering into the city of joy.

We're talking about some very basic survival skills, skills of finding and keeping a job, skills of succeeding in education, skills of choosing a mate, and skills of helping young people learn to understand themselves. If you disciple them properly, you will have helped them to see that it is not a matter of either/or; survival is the road to success, not just a substitute for success.

Jesus said, "Love your neighbor as yourself." As *yourself*. There is nothing urban young people need more than the ability to love themselves. Only then will they be capable of loving others. The city tends to do one of two things to young people. It will either destroy their ability to love themselves, or it will tempt them with countless chances to indulge in a selfish self-love. Neither enables them to carry out Jesus' commandment.

Survival Is Linked to Self-Image

Without a feeling of self-worth, no one can successfully confront the tough affairs of life. To survive and succeed, young people have to be able to say, "Hey, I'm worth something. I matter. I'm basically OK." Of course Christians believe that no one can be totally OK without faith in Jesus Christ, but nothing should or can ultimately separate believers from the love of Christ. That's a fact. But it's a fact that many young people can't feel.

One thing you can do to make youth feel their worth in Christ is to involve them in activities that deal meaningfully with their environment and affirm their worth. Relate the gospel, through your activities, to their world. Strive to show that Christ walks on the pavement among the tenements and not just along the tree-shaded streets of the suburbs.

You also develop a feeling of worth in young people by training them to communicate their faults and fears. You want to teach them to resist sin but also to confess it without fear. By listening, understanding, and forgiving, you become someone they can trust. "Do unto others as you would have them do to you," Jesus commanded. In the city, though, it is often easier (and seemingly safer) just to hide your feelings and fears and "do unto others before they do unto you." If you live out the Golden Rule before their eyes, you will make it much easier for them to imitate the Christlike way of dealing with others.

Our Image With Others

This issue of relationships is a very important one in the lives of urban young people, and unfortunately it's an issue we in the church haven't always dealt with very well. Much of our teaching about the family and relationships within it assumes that all children come from stable two-parent families. In making such an assumption, we've ignored the obvious fact that many urban young people come from homes with one parent or no parents. In ministering to the individual young person, begin by accepting whatever the reality of his home life is. You will help the young person to "survive and succeed" in that home if you assure him of your loving acceptance in the midst of the home situation. How can you encourage a teen to love his family with a Christlike love, if you have failed even to accept the reality of the home?

One morning I had breakfast with a young lady who had been having a great deal of difficulty in her home. Her relationship with her parents was strained, and because of this she had bad relationships with her peers and displayed a generally negative attitude toward life. As I persuaded her to accept the situation at home, she became more positive. This spilled into her friendships and home life, as she accepted her parents and let Christ into her home.

Young people should be encouraged to work within the family system. Responsibility has a lot to do with learning to work in and through systems. The home is a system, and young people should be encouraged to help others in the family with homework, chores, and preparations for special family events. And they should be trained to see that in certain situations others will need them simply to listen to them as they talk through specific problems.

Guiding Teens

We might expand on this discussion of relationships by looking at those timeless concerns young people have—dating, courtship, and marriage. The older we get, the easier it is for us to forget the intensity young people feel when they confront these issues. Black or white, urban or rural, rich or poor—young people consider dating and marriage to be life-and-death matters. Even if we had nothing else to go on, a look at statistics about teenage pregnancies and divorce should convince us of the need for church counseling and teaching about these issues.

One practical way you can help is to show the young person the difference between courtship and friendship. Youth need to see a date as it is defined—"an appointment between members of the opposite sex"—and not something more than that. Many young people face problems because they confuse dating and courtship, taking dating too seriously and courtship too lightly. Few things you as a youth worker do are of as much importance as this matter of training the young person to seek a lifelong mate with wisdom and faith.

We now need to move from the grand to the nitty-gritty. We need to consider some of the skills urban young people often lack and some of the training they too rarely receive. All too frequently, urban young people have gotten little or no help in developing the simple skills needed to manage life, to survive day by day. I'm speaking here of such things as budgeting, using a checkbook, shopping, eating nutritionally, purchasing insurance, and choosing and furnishing a residence. Because urban schools and homes frequently fail to fulfill their responsibilities to train young people in these areas, the church, through its youth ministry, can and should fill the vacuum.

In addition to working with young people on developing such skills for managing daily responsibilities, the youth worker can also assist in the broader areas of education and employment. Leadership in these areas should preferably come from a person trained in some area of education—Christian or public—but each youth worker can play a part by encouraging young people and by helping to organize and run such things as seminars on study skills, tutorial services in reading and math, and workshops on leadership. Urban youth also need basic advice on how to get and keep a job. It's a fact of life that young people need to know certain things to survive in the working world of the "system." It's all too easy for untrained youth to make foolish decisions about attendance, dress, and attitudes toward work. In making those foolish decisions, they can seriously damage their chances to get or keep a job.

Success in Perspective

> Do not let this Book of the Law depart from your mouth; meditate on it day and night, so that you may be careful to do everything written in it. Then you will be prosperous and successful.
>
> *Joshua 1:8*

This verse reminds us in a timely way that our success depends ultimately on the nature of our relationship to the Word of God. When I think of success for Christians, I think of the handling of our affairs so as to produce social, personal, and spiritual peace. This definition assumes that such peace comes from the knowledge of God's forgiveness and the hope of His salvation. But in defining peace this way, I am also thinking of more practical things, such as the peace we feel when we have succeeded in setting goals and reaching them. No matter how spiritually sensitive we are, we find it hard to be at peace with ourselves when our lives seem like endless records of failures rather than successes.

We might do well to look at the relationship of survival and success this way—it's foolish to try to achieve success without having learned the ways of survival, but survival alone is not what God wants for us. Imagine God's desire for us to have adequate shelter. He'd think us terribly foolish, wouldn't He, if we bought expensive furniture and appliances but failed to put a roof over our heads or outer walls around our rooms? That's success without true survival. But in a similar way, how can we imagine God wanting us to live in the roughest shell of a house, with little or nothing on the inside?

Society equates success too exclusively with money and power. Reacting against that, we tend to discourage young people from dreaming big dreams and wanting big things. Sometimes we take the good and necessary caution against crass materialism to the extreme and subconsciously will poverty on our children.

Jesus did not will poverty and repeated failure on those who loved Him; neither did He extol the virtues of the denarius—but He did come to offer release to the poor. Quoting Isaiah, and applying the prophecy to himself, Jesus said,

> . . . he has anointed me
>   to preach good news to the poor.
> He has sent me to proclaim freedom for the prisoners
>   and recovery of sight for the blind.
> *Luke 4:18*

Your young people need to hear that message. God wants the best for all His people, no matter what their economic status.

In practical terms, how does God give young people His best? Let's look at the matter of tithing for an example. From an early age, Christian young people should be taught the principles of giving cheerfully to God and trusting Him to give abundantly in return. The New Testament teaches us that "the righteous will live by faith" (Romans 1:17). Such a statement implies that every good gift is from the Father, given to us through His grace by our faith in Christ, His Word.

Though it may appear absurd to talk about poverty-stricken urban young people tithing, it really isn't. Even the smallest amount of money they can give is significant, and if they have no money to give to the Lord's work they can learn to give of their time and talents. If we were discussing merely worldly success at this point, then all our talk about giving might seem ridiculous. But our discussion makes sense because we're talking about the drastic difference in values between the Christian and non-Christian; the non-Christian takes and takes and takes, while the Christian gives and receives out of God's grace.

The church can also train young people for success by working to provide advice and assistance in the areas of jobs and education. No doubt your church has a good number of resources—businessmen and women, skilled tradesmen, blue-collar workers, and professionals—

waiting to be tapped. Use these lay people as speakers, teachers, or mentors to give assistance to needy young people. You can also help by providing money and transportation to enable youth to visit a college campus or job site. Help young people to make the necessary contacts and gain the necessary exposure. More often than not, they will already know their needs for employment and education. The most important thing you can do is to provide them with valuable resources and encouragement.

In today's job market, muscle power is becoming less and less important. Brain power is the wave of the future. Your young people will need training in high technology more than ever before. Factory jobs in urban areas will become fewer and fewer—look to the auto industry as an example. Robots have replaced humans in some cases. Your young people need to learn computer technology to keep up with future opportunities. As you see ways to introduce them to these situations, do so.

Don't expect your seeds of encouragement to be ready for harvest overnight. In many ways, your work with young people on career planning should begin in the early elementary years. You don't, of course, offer a third grader a seminar on methods of interviewing! But from an early age young people need to see Christians who are interested in their future. They also need to have caring, knowledgeable people helping them to identify skills and interests. If someone has obvious abilities in a certain area (music, math, medicine), then she needs encouragement and support in that direction; if someone has an obvious need in a certain area, then special tutorial work will be in order. There is no set rule at work here, except the command of the Lord that tells you to love your neighbor—that down-and-out urban youth—as yourself.

If he doesn't believe in and love himself, a young person will usually not have the motivation, let alone the means, to survive and succeed. He needs to know that someone who survived and succeeded in spite of incredible odds—Jesus—loves him very much. Just as the grave itself couldn't contain and conquer Jesus, neither should the ghetto be able to destroy the urban young person. To succeed, that young person must first be released from bondage, the bondage of fear and guilt. From beginning to end, your work with that youth must be undergirded by the reality and power of the gospel of Jesus Christ. God longs for His children to survive and succeed. "For God did not give us a spirit of timidity, but a spirit of power, of love and of self-discipline" (2 Timothy 1:7).

LIFE RESPONSE

1. Survival and success are linked to self-image. You can help your teens see that a positive self-image (not a defeated or arrogant one) can help them survive and succeed in their world.

Choose two articulate teens to be your partners. Put three chairs in the middle of the room, and sit facing each other. Assign three parts. One of you will be a defeated teen with a negative self-image. Another will be the arrogant one, with a terribly inflated self-image. The last (and don't you take this part) will be the self-assured teen, comfortable and at ease with herself.

Choose an imaginary situation, but one that might actually occur at school, on the streets, or at home. Bounce comments off each other from your assigned perspective. Close it off when you've had fun with this and clarified positions.

In the group, explore the idea of self-image as related to survival. Ask your group to give the characters descriptive names. What is each like? Who is most attractive? Why? Who would you vote most likely to succeed? Why? How does all this make you feel?

2. All teens are concerned with dating and marriage. Urban teens, in particular, see a conglomeration of male/female roles and relationships, many of them negative. The following exercise should bring the issues out in the open.

Choose a boy/girl pair to play the roles of a married couple. Have them ask each other the following questions in front of the group. Each will answer from his or her own perspective.

- What are the three most important items in our budget?
- What bothers you most about money?
- What do you like best and dislike most about where we live?
- Should married people be best friends? Why or why not?
- How do you feel about our time dating together?

Stop the role playing and ask the group to identify the differences in points of view that have come up. Ask what group members want out of marriage. Ask how they might identify positive partners through dating.

Chapter Six

Caring for the Whole Person

IT'S A FUNNY and yet sad thing, this habit we have of twisting Scripture to make it say things the Lord never intended. One of the verses I most often hear distorted is Philippians 4:13. The *New English Bible* gives it this way: "I have strength for anything through him who gives me power." (The King James Version says, "I can do all things through Christ which strengtheneth me.")

Now I've often heard fellow Christians quote this verse in a way that would lead you to believe that once you become a Christian, *presto!* you have no more human needs, weaknesses, or limits. But in reality, no amount of superficial and loose "God talk" can hide the fact that, after all, we still are creatures who need many things if we are to grow and prosper. It will do us absolutely no good to pretend otherwise, so in this chapter I want to talk about some of those common needs and explore ways of meeting them.

Working with young people is like building a house. Based upon a foundation of spiritual values, you try to meet their needs by building a structure around them that they can rely on to show them how they should live and equip them to live that way. The intellectual, relational, and social structures you build are like the roof of the house; the occupational and marital structures are like its walls. We need to become "wise master builders," using the best tools and resources available to us (computer-taught reading skills, job training programs, and interview techniques, for example). Many groups are vying for the mind and imagination of young people.

Needs and the Christian

Without a doubt, most important is the universal need for love and security. Through sin, human beings have become alienated from God and each other. In an earlier chapter I said some positive things about the city and about the image of the believer's final home as one large, redeemed city, but now I need to say something of a different nature. We notice in the Bible that the first city was founded by Cain, history's first murderer on record. This biblical story about the founding of the very first city gets at a deep truth about cities, and especially our huge modern cities. The truth is that cities are places of great alienation where people frequently experience painful separation from God, from nature, and from other people. To fill the need for love that overcomes alienation, many in the city will offer young people counterfeit things—illicit sex, drugs, and violence. You must acknowledge this great need in your teenagers, and with God's grace, you must seek to fulfill it in healthy and proper ways.

Young people need to be taught moral values and how to clarify such values in particular settings and situations. Many of them, for example, need to be shown the destructive potential of drugs, alcohol, and sexual promiscuity. The world of the street will do its best to destroy a kid's character and integrity. But by using some of the methods I've outlined in other portions of this book, you can help to fortify youth from attack.

The apostle Paul calls the human body the temple of the Holy Spirit. If we abuse our own bodies, doesn't it follow that we will find it difficult, perhaps impossible, to avoid abusing others? If we hate ourselves, we will most likely hate others. Your effort to instruct young people in moral values must go hand in hand with an attempt to build up their self-esteem. You are arming them against the assaults of Satan, who wants them to doubt themselves so that they come to doubt God's grace.

In an ideal world, you would attempt to meet young people's needs by working in tandem with family and community. But in reality, you will find yourself working alone, at times, because the family or immediate community has failed to fulfill its obligations. You can attempt to fill this vacuum by making use of small groups, special clubs within the church, team activities, and rap sessions to provide the sense of fellowship and acceptance these young people lack. The rap session, in particular, provides an excellent opportunity for getting young people to struggle with the question of how their values relate to the many tough realities of urban life. You don't want to try to replace their families, but you can provide a group setting in which they feel free to struggle with questions of values they might not be able to raise in their homes or communities.

Urban young people can easily feel isolated and lonely, that life is passing them by, that they are nothing but feeble streams trickling alongside the rushing torrent of American life. They need to be taught to see that all of God's children—black and white, European and native

American, rich and poor—are equally important streams flowing into that larger rushing river of God's community, His people. Such a view will give them a true respect for their own origins along with those of others.

We come full circle when we look at a final need, the need for young people to know their strength in Christ. "I can do everything through him who gives me strength" (Philippians 4:13). I hope at this point we can see this verse properly. To have strength you don't have to deny your needs. Indeed, one of the strengths Christ gives to believers is the power to know that they don't have to feel guilty about those needs. The message of the gospel—one of forgiveness and hope—fortifies young people for their battles with Satan and self.

Needs and Young People

In determining how we can best go about meeting those needs, we begin with the issue of awareness. A doctor would never think of operating on a patient without knowing the precise nature of his illness and quite a bit about the his medical history. In a similar way, a youth worker should not attempt to "operate" on a young person without having gained necessary insight into urban culture and ethnic life in general, and into the specific urban environment of his group.

Ideally, a youth worker's training would include classroom teaching, a good deal of reading, and organized "field" experience in an urban environment. To organize such training effectively, you may need to get several churches to join together in such an undertaking. In any case, it is crucial for you to receive training from educators, pastors, and psychologists who have an intimate knowledge of urban young people and their environment. A youth worker also needs to be an ardent student of the

Scriptures. He needs to begin and maintain a regular study of the Scriptures for knowledge and guidance.

To teenagers, love is spelled T-I-M-E. If you don't have any to give, you're telling them you don't care. While large meetings provide you better opportunities for conveying what you believe, individual appointments allow you to demonstrate. They also allow you to "custom fit" Christianity to the teenager's life and problems. A teenager opens up in an appointment like nowhere else, allowing for honest feedback in both directions. Because teens can see that you do more than just preach at them, real discipleship can take place.

Here are some guidelines for meeting with teens one-on-one:

1. Prayerfully seek an attitude of relying on God's wisdom and leading rather than a puffed-up belief that you can solve the person's problems. In a spirit of humility, realize that you also have unsolved problems and recognize yourself as another sinful human being just like the teen with whom you are working. Don't limit your praying to before the appointment; pray during it as well, constantly asking God what to say—or not say—next.

2. Respond to what the person is saying and feeling, not to where you want her to be. Let the young person begin where she feels comfortable; respond to her there. Then she will feel more comfortable moving into more meaningful issues. If she senses that you know and care where she is at first, then she will have enough trust in you to enable her to share more difficult items with you. Avoid stereotyping. Don't force the person to make a spiritual commitment if she's not ready.

3. Accept the person just the way he is. This doesn't mean that you have to like everything about him. It does mean that you allow him the freedom to be himself.

He doesn't have to be the way you want him to be. Respecting him enough to allow him to be the way he is will do much to relieve his fear of being condemned and rejected by you.

4. Be as open and honest as possible with your responses to her. You may be the only person who loves and respects her enough to give her an accurate picture of how she comes across to others. If you are open about your own experiences and feelings, she can gain a realistic picture of what the Christian life is. Your honesty may prevent future disillusionment with Christianity. It will also show her how to be honest.

5. Listen intently to what the teen is saying and how he is responding in the situation. Be alert and aware of what he is doing, and also be sensitive to your own feelings and reactions for him. Empathize and feel with the person rather than trying to analyze him. Pay close attention to both verbal and nonverbal behavior (voice intonation and rate, eyes watering, skin flushing, gestures, body position). Learn to trust your hunches about what the person is doing, and have the courage to check them out. Ask him if your perception is correct. One of the most important processes in communicating effectively is listening carefully.

6. All you have in any counseling relationship is yourself. Your skills and techniques are only as good as you are effective in building healthy relationships. So be a human being; have the courage to be imperfect. Young people are much more willing to talk meaningfully with a warm-blooded person with whom they can identify than they are with a lofty image of perfection and saintliness. Be open to give and receive both positive and negative feedback.

7. Try to help the young person learn how to solve her problems and make her own decisions. Teach her that

she can depend on her own God-given brains and character. Don't feed your own ego by fostering her dependency on you. You are not a canned answer machine or a dispenser of prepackaged frozen problem-solving formulas. Help her to become independently dependent on Jesus Christ.

8. Integrate prayer into your conversation in a way that shows the young person that God is concerned and can help. But do not use prayer as an easy answer or as a "cop-out" for not working with the person at a deeper level where he is really hurting.

9. It is important to remember that all behavior is purposeful. Do not discount seemingly silly and pointless behavior as unimportant. Try to help the young person understand which of these goals (acceptance from others, feelings of power or importance, revenge, attention, self-concealment, etc.) she is really striving for. Help her evaluate her goals and then encourage her to develop more constructive behaviors and habit patterns for achieving them.

10. Be aware of your abilities and capacities as a youth worker. Don't be afraid to stretch yourself by working in difficult counseling situations. Remember, though, that you are working with valuable human beings. When you think you are beyond the limits of your present abilities, don't hesitate to refer the individual to someone you think is more qualified (another staff member, minister, school counselor, psychologist, or medical doctor). Tell the person why you are making the referral and help him make the transition in any way you can.

Act More Than React

In a healthy youth ministry, the educated one—the youth worker—will inevitably become the educator.

You probably have had a physical exam in which the doctor strikes your knee with a rubber mallet to test your reflexes. Your leg sits motionless until the mallet hits, and then—*pop!*—there's a jerk of the leg. All too often our youth ministries are like that. We don't act, we only react; we don't try to prevent crises, we only react to them when they occur.

A better way for us to deal with many of the crises of young people is to try to equip them with biblical principles that will help them to anticipate and deal with their own problems. As a youth worker, you should have had some training in how to organize workshops, films, and field trips to train your young people. For example, think of the great potential value of an organized trip to a hospital, prison, youth home, or courtroom. Most urban youth have only negative associations or contacts with such institutions. An educational trip to one of these places could help to put the institution into perspective for the young person.

Some problems can't be prevented. They must be encountered with sensitivity and strength when they occur. At this point—at the time of crisis—the youth worker's role as counselor and adviser becomes important.

In Galatians 6:2, Paul tells us to "carry each other's burdens, and in this way you will fulfil the law of Christ." One of a young person's greatest needs is to know that someone cares and understands. Remember when you were a little child and awoke from a bad dream in the middle of the night? You cried out for your mom or dad, didn't you? No doubt one of them came to comfort you and listen to your fears. What would you have thought about their love if neither had come? If you can remember such an experience, you can perhaps understand what it's like for a lonely young person to cry out and get no response, to fear that no one on earth or in Heaven hears.

Just by being there for the young person, you can demonstrate God's active, searching love. I use the word "searching" because trouble doesn't always deposit itself on our doorstep in search of help. We must often search out those who need loving care.

As one who works with young people, you must learn how to read the unintentional signs of distress they give. Look for such things as sudden changes in habits or violent swings of mood; obvious attention-getting behavior; overindulgence in eating, drinking, or sexual activity; and frequent dishonesty. If you spot such signals— which seem to cry out, "I need help!"—then you should proceed by establishing genuine contact and rapport with the youth.

Invite him out for something to eat. Hear the young person out, but don't expect to have immediate answers to every dilemma. After all, some of these problems have been 15 years in the making, so you can't expect to solve each one in one or two meetings. In fact, if you rush into things too fast, you may destroy whatever trust the young person has developed toward you. Take it easy, be patient, and let him know how much you genuinely care. And don't—unless you fear for the youth's physical or mental safety—bring up his problem with others. If you do, you may quickly lose the teen's trust.

Assuming you have gained the young person's trust and are able to keep it, what can you specifically do? It's important for you to allow the young person great freedom in expressing himself. Let the teenager cry, laugh, or express anger. Listen. Let him talk about the problem until he begins to see new things about it and its possible solution.

I personally favor a method of counseling that keeps the youth worker as much as possible out of the business of dishing out advice. Sometimes you will want to direct the young person's thoughts and offer a timely passage of Scripture or bit of advice, but in general I advocate an approach that stresses being there in Christ for that young person.

There will come times when you encounter problems in your young people that somehow seem beyond you. At that point don't hesitate to refer such a problem to a professional staff worker or the pastor of your church. It's important throughout, however, to keep such things as confidential as possible.

Young people need not only to know that you stand there ready to help, but also that you care enough to keep their problems private.

Up to this point, I have neglected a subject we frequently neglect in our youth work—fun. Play and laughter offer the young person an unparalleled chance to release frustrations and forget some of their nagging, constant worries. Young people need recreation as much as they need counseling and education. Try to organize such things as songfests, athletic activities, camp-outs, or monthly birthday parties.

In poor communities, the youth ministry may have to pick up the tab for many of these events. In some instances the young people can participate in fund-raising car washes and the like to earn the money to pay for the activity. In any case, the money and time invested in providing simple fun for the young person are well spent.

I've just provided a basic outline for a youth ministry oriented toward fulfilling needs. Use this as a foundation and build on it with your own effort and ingenuity. Be creative and persistent. Try new approaches and follow through on them. In doing so you will help to satisfy young people's spiritual hunger. And more importantly, you will help direct them to the One who is the true and everlasting Bread of Life.

LIFE RESPONSE

1. The city is a place where many young people feel alienated from God, nature, and others. Your youth group can be a part of overcoming the effects of alienation by encouraging its members to affirm one another.

Pair off your youth and give everyone a piece of paper and pen or pencil. Ask them to think about the good qualities they've seen in their partner. Have them jot a note describing one good quality they've noticed. Then ask each pair to share their partner's good quality with the group and exchange notes of affirmation.

2. The youth group can and should be a place where teens share their struggles and receive support. You undoubtedly have rap sessions on specific topics already. Try throwing the session wide open. A prompting question could be, "How do I feel about my identity as a Christian teen?"

Be prepared for a flood of responses once people begin expressing themselves. Your guideline as moderator is to try to elicit supportive comments from other group members. A good prompting question is, "What strengths do the rest of you see in (the speaker) that would help (him or her) deal with that?"

3. Schedule trips to a hospital, prison, youth home, or courtroom. On your return, discuss with your teens what they saw or heard that was new to them in a positive way. Ask how their views may have changed. Talk about the importance of the institution for society.

Chapter Seven

Bible in Life

AS THEY GET into the work of ministering to young people, Christians inevitably ask the question, "What resources are available to me to make my work more efficient and effective?" We could list many things—films, books, concerts, games, and the like—but we'd be making the most serious mistake possible if we did not put the Bible at the top of our list. This Book, the living, active Word of God, is the greatest resource available to a youth worker. But it's not just a tool you use. It's a Word spoken, challenging and reassuring you.

I'll say it simply: if you don't have a proper relationship to the Bible as resource and Word, you will not have a dynamic youth ministry. You may be able to have occasional high points and exciting moments in your ministry, but only a deep relationship with God's Word will enable you to have a sustained and lively outreach.

Remember that the Bible is a historical document. Like all history, it tells a story, in this case the great story of God's dealings with human beings. As Christians, we take it as a matter of faith that God's Holy

Spirit guided and inspired those who wrote the books of Scripture. If you are to use the Bible, it is important for you and your young people to understand these basic facts Christians believe about it.

The Road Map of God's Love

As we move into a specific discussion of the Bible's relevance and impact, it may help us to think of it as a road map.

The typical urban teenager—unaware of her ultimate "roots," insecure about present life, and completely unsure about the future—desperately needs such a road map. When she reads and understands the Scriptures, it's like taking a helicopter flight far above the city. From the air, the teen gets a new perspective, seeing how her small block fits into a larger picture of streets, buildings, parks, and freeways. Similarly, the Scriptures give perspective, as they show us how our individual lives fit into the picture of God's plan for the world. Let's now take a brief journey through those Scriptures, outlining the road map of God's love.

Logically enough, the Bible begins at the very beginning. It tells us of God's creation and the origin of sin in rebellion against God. The Lord prepares the way for salvation and reconciliation by choosing the nation Israel to be His special people.

Beginning with Abraham, Isaac, and Jacob, God reveals that He intends to bring a Savior to redeem mankind. Exodus tells us of the Israelites' enslavement in Egypt and of their release from bondage through the leadership of Moses. We also learn in these early books of the Old Testament about Israel's wanderings in the desert, where they receive God's law and learn to worship and know Him. They wander for 40 years in the desert, and finally enter the promised land of Canaan under the leadership of Joshua.

Israel's story continues in the Books of Judges and Ruth. At times, the people and their leaders obey God and remain faithful to Him, and at times they fail to follow Him. God always remains faithful to His people, even when He punishes them.

In 1 Samuel, we read of Israel becoming a kingdom, first under the rule of Saul, then under David. As David and Solomon rule, Israel reaches the peak of its power and influence. David writes many of the Psalms, and his son Solomon continues the glorious reign over Israel and also writes most of the Book of Proverbs.

But then comes decline, as the kingdom splits into two parts. Most of the kings of both Israel and Judah turn away from God. Most of the warnings from the Lord's prophets fall on deaf ears, as the rulers of Israel and Judah ignore God's warnings. Eventually, more powerful nations overrun the Hebrew kingdoms, and God's people find themselves taken away to be servants to their conquerors (2 Kings).

Many years later, God revives His people, using Nehemiah and Ezra as His leaders to restore Jerusalem. The Old Testament ends as God's prophets tell His people where they have failed and prophesy (more than 400 years before Christ's birth) about the coming of a Savior.

The New Testament begins with the Christmas event and the life of Jesus. From slightly different angles, each of the four Gospels—Matthew, Mark, Luke, and John—tells the story of Jesus' birth, life, death, and resurrection. Jesus, they tell us, has fulfilled God's plan for human history. When He died on the cross, He took upon himself the punishment for human sin. And when He rose to new life, He gave new life to all who follow Him.

The Book of Acts relates the story of Christ's followers who begin His church after the Master has returned to Heaven.

The remainder of the New Testament is made up of the letters of the church's leaders—Paul, John, Peter, James, and Jude. These letters, or epistles, explain and apply the gospel to specific situations.

Logically, the Bible ends at the very end. The Book of Revelation looks forward to the return of Christ, the end of earthly history, and the church's eternal life with Christ forever.

Following the Way

As essential as such a basic knowledge of the Scriptures is, it is hardly sufficient. Young people have to see the Bible as something more than a collection of interesting stories about people long dead. They have to hear the Bible, hear it as God's Word spoken to them. The writer of the letter to the Hebrews put it well: "The word of God is living and active. Sharper than any double-edged sword, it penetrates even to dividing soul and spirit, joints and marrow" (Hebrews 4:12).

If we fail to see the life in Scripture, we make the same mistake as the Pharisees, of whom Jesus said in John 5:39, 40. "You diligently study the Scriptures because you think that by them you possess eternal life. These are the Scriptures that testify about me, yet you refuse to come to me to have life." The pages of Scripture point to Him, Jesus says; in those pages He reveals himself, not only information about himself.

This is what makes the Scriptures alive, active, dynamic. In them, God reveals himself in language that we can understand and find relevant to our individual situations. The Holy Spirit brought the Scriptures into being (2 Peter 1:20, 21), and He makes them come alive for the believer today. Christians who find the Bible dull simply have not understood it for what it is.

If this is true—what I've said about the Scriptures being an alive and active Word addressed to us today—what kind of responses are we called to make? For one, we should assume that God expects and hopes for a response of thanksgiving from us for His communication. We know from the Scriptures themselves how delighted God is by our worship and praise. David speaks eloquently about this:

> Oh, how I love your law!
>   I meditate on it all day long. . . .
> May my lips overflow with praise,
>   for you teach me your decrees. . . .
> Let me live that I may praise you,
>   and may your laws sustain me.
> *Psalm 119:97, 171, 175*

A second way we should respond to the Scriptures is to be convicted of our sin. That passage from Hebrews, you remember, speaks of the Word as a sword. It goes on to say that that sword cuts through our defenses to expose us as we really are. In one sense, the Bible is an intruder that breaks into the private areas that we've tried to hide from God.

If you are open to the Bible and its message, it will be impossible for you to read it without recognizing your sinful nature and feeling remorse over it. Yet as soon as the Bible tells us of our sinfulness, it also brings us a message of forgiveness. In 1 John 1:9 God puts into writing His promise that He is faithful and does forgive our sins.

God also calls us to obedience through His Word. In 2 Timothy 3:16, 17, we read that "All Scripture is God-breathed and is useful for . . . correcting and training in righteousness, so that the man of God may be thoroughly equipped for every good work." You and those you disciple should be trained to hear in the Word of God a call to action. James says it well in the New Testament when he confronts us: "You believe that there is one God. Good! Even the demons believe that—and shudder. . . . Faith by itself, if it is not accompanied by action, is dead" (James 2:19, 17). Through our practical obedience, we express to God and others our love of Christ and our gratitude for His grace.

The Bible in Everyday Life

Some say the Bible isn't practical, but I say what can be more practical than changed lives? Like all things that come from God, the Bible gives life. Through the Word of Scripture, God gives life by speaking to teens about their most basic concerns—family, friendships, sex, money, and marriage—and it doesn't just talk about these things; it gives the teen direction in dealing with them.

In my own ministry, I don't seek to produce a batch of junior theologians or junior ministers. I'm more interested to see young people take hold of the Word of God and apply it to their lives.

At various times in my life, I have been bothered by bad habits that have bound me. In those times I've gone to the Bible, asking the Holy Spirit to help me escape from the prison of my own desires. Sometimes God has only needed to use a verse or two to meet my need. At other times I've had to struggle longer with questions of my identity and with my insecurity. But even in my longest struggles, I've been assured by God's Word that He loves me and that He has given me unique gifts to use in His service.

Sometimes we need nothing more than a quick word of encouragement or challenge, while at others we need profound, deeper support. I've found support through the Scriptures often simply by realizing that they must have great significance, because God cares enough for me to speak to me through His Word.

If young people are to have a meaningful time reading God's Word, they must be able to make these connections of the Bible with the crucial problems of life. We speak of such times with the Word as "devotional times," but what exactly does that phrase mean? What is supposed to happen during one of these devotional times?

First of all, young people's values should be strengthened. Let's say they are tempted to steal or cheat. The Scriptures offer comfort and encouragement. Finding this, teens will feel more secure in God, and if they feel more secure in God, they will be much less likely to cave in to such temptations.

Young people should be able to learn the will of God through devotional times. There is no set answer to the question "How do I learn the will of God?" but I think it safe to say that God uses His Word to challenge us when we've strayed from His will and to give us peace and assurance when we've held fast to it. More than anything, teens should be able to take away from their devotional times a sense that they can fulfill the expectations God has mapped out for them in Scripture.

If teens are going to accomplish these things in their devotional times, they must be trained to deal with Scripture at the level of image rather than vague abstractions and bare facts. In every section of the Word, concepts are inseparable from word pictures, stories, and characters. Teens can take an image in Scripture—like the Christian as an athlete in 2 Timothy 2:5 or Jesus as a servant in Philippians 2:7—and draw out or relate its meaning for their own experience. At the end of this chapter, I've provided examples of this devotional process at work. You may want to try one of them with your own group.

Because Bible study must play a crucial role in an urban youth ministry, you need to keep some things in mind as you make use of the Scriptures in your ministry. The first has to do with the atmosphere in which you try to train young people in the Scriptures. It should be warm, loving, friendly, and accepting. Teaching the Scriptures is a serious matter, but you're not going to help yourself by losing your temper at a kid who's fooling around.

You'll find it easier to teach in a smaller group with as few distractions as possible. To eliminate those annoying interruptions, choose a private room rather than an open area. If you don't have a separate area, pick a corner of the room and have the group face the corner. Put potentially distracting things away.

In the actual teaching process, you should never lose sight of your young people's needs and never fail to know what your aim in the study is. Most young people need direction; they need to have goals even in a process as apparently simple as a group study of the Bible. But once we've said that about goals, we need to add a word about the process itself. Never fix your mind on distant goals to the degree that you fail to teach sensitively in the present from real-life experiences.

You may find role playing helpful in teaching the Bible and relating it to such real-life experiences. Get several members of your group involved in acting out a story from the Bible. Such involvement forces the young person into a deeper consideration of such things as feelings, conflicts, and decision making.

Imagine the young person who has just finished playing the role of Abraham, as he struggles with the command to sacrifice his son, Isaac. Not only is that young person going to have to struggle with the conflict between God's will and human love, but he is also going to feel closer to the Bible characters because of the way their struggles resemble his. In feeling closer to the characters, the teen feels closer to the Word of God, being able to hear it as a word spoken in his particular situation.

The Mechanics

Try to give your young people a modern translation of the Bible to use, because that will make your lesson more understandable. For study with young people, I suggest such versions as the *New International Version* (NIV), *New American Standard Bible* (NASB), *The Living Bible* (TLB), and *Today's English Version* (TEV).

The youth worker should try to supply each member of the group with a Bible. It helps a great deal for urban youth to have a new Bible given to them; a tattered, used copy of the Scriptures may well seem like just another hand-me-down, another crumb from the table of the more fortunate. But that new Bible can serve as a message, saying, "You're worthy! God cares about you, and so do we."

Now let's take a look at some examples of how to guide your teens to the study of Scripture at the image level. You can try these in the group setting or copy them for handout use so individuals can use them at home.

Image Exercises

We all have heard how professional athletes, movie stars, and recording artists live. Many of us have been envious at times. In 2 Timothy 2:1-7, Paul is writing to his friend Timothy about the manner of life he and all Christians should adopt. Read the passage twice.

1. How is Timothy supposed to be "strong in the grace" (v. 1)? Grace is the life and power of God given to you. What would you think if someone were to tell you to be "strong in the grace that is in Christ Jesus"?

2. What was Timothy instructed to do with what he had learned from Paul (v. 2)? Is this process happening in your church? Are you part of the process?

3. Describe the life of the soldier (vv. 3, 4). Are you "entangled" in any way? Can you change this? Look at the armor of the soldier in Christ (Ephesians 6:10-18).

4. In what ways was Paul himself like the athlete in v. 5? Read 2 Timothy 4:7, 8 to get another insight on Paul. He was almost at the end of his life when he wrote this.

5. Describe the farmer's life. What does v. 6 tell you? What does it mean for you to work hard as a Christian?

As a Christian you belong to a large family of God, whose members are to love one another as Jesus loves them. In Philippians 1:3-11, Paul is writing to the Christians in the city of Philippi. He discusses the nature of this love Christians have for each other. Read the passage twice.

1. How does Paul claim to feel toward these Christians (vv. 7, 8)? Do you know Christians who feel this way toward one another? What is the secret as to how they do it?

2. Why does Paul feel so confident (v. 6)? How is God working in your life? How can you tell?

3. Love involves more than "good feelings." It also involves knowledge (v. 9) and the search for good and excellent things (v. 10). What does this tell you about the way you get along with your family and friends?

4. What is the day of Christ (vv. 6, 10)? Do you look forward to it? What difference should it make to you today?

Can you see any difference between yourself and your non-Christian friends? Psalm 1, a song to God, contrasts the wicked and righteous. Look for yourself in it as you try to draw out lessons for everyday living. Read the psalm through twice.

1. How does the Psalm describe the righteous person (vv. 1-3)? Does it remind you of anyone you know? Who? Why?

2. Where do you run into the "counsel of the wicked" (v. 1)? How can you avoid being influenced by it? Why will you be blessed if you do so?

3. How are you, the follower of God, like a tree (v. 3)?

4. The wicked person is like chaff, the husk of a seed (v. 4). What does this tell you about the world's way of living?

5. Why do we need to meditate on God's Word each day (v. 2)? What would you need to do in order to start doing this yourself?

LIFE RESPONSE

1. Many Christians know Bible stories, but have little idea how they fit together. What they lack is the big picture—God's road map from beginning to end.

Read again the section at the beginning of this chapter, "The Road Map of God's Love." Read this section aloud to your group, or better yet, put the story in your own words.

Meanwhile, have one of your teens trace the road on butcher paper, marking especially the major stopping points. Discuss with your teens the resulting biblical overview. What new things did they learn? How has their perception of the Bible grown? Leave the road map posted in your meeting place.

2. One of the most important things you can do for your young people is help them see the Bible for what it is—a vital and active Word addressed to us today. To help drive home this point with your teens, have them memorize David's words from Psalm 119:97, 171, and 175 as quoted on page 85. You might encourage this by setting up teams to see who can memorize the fastest. Team members help each other learn the passage until every person on the team can recite it. The first team to have all members recite the verse from memory wins.

3. Choose a translation you want to use regularly, and make sure every teen in your group has a copy. Raise the money with teen projects. Businessmen and women in your church may have contacts to help you organize. Encourage teens to contribute their fund-raising ideas. Then go out, raise the money, and buy those Bibles!

Chapter Eight

Modeling Christ

FOR A MINUTE, imagine something with me. Imagine that you are the friend of someone who is going to build a very large structure—say the Sears Tower in Chicago, the World Trade Center in New York, or the Superdome in New Orleans. He comes to you just before he is to begin work, and he tells you that he has not bothered to have any plans or drawings made up. He plans to "wing it," he says, making up the design as he goes along.

What will you do? Laugh? Cry? Head for the phone to call the authorities?

No matter what any one of us might do in such a situation, I am sure we would find his foolishness a very serious thing. We'd think his carelessness to be an awful matter, especially considering the complexity of any major structure. Yet how many of us even pause to think about a need for planning when we set out to disciple a young person in the ways of Jesus Christ? We'd think a person crazy if he began work on a building without plans, but we might not raise a question at all if he were to go into the process of discipling without planning.

A Plan for Discipleship

The apostle Paul says clearly that God waited until just the right time before sending His Son into the world for our salvation. The same Paul tells us that God's plan for individual human life was formed before the very foundations of the earth. Before He ascended to the Father, Jesus sent His own disciples out to preach and disciple others, commanding them: "Therefore go and make disciples of all nations, baptizing them in the name of the Father and of the Son and of the Holy Spirit" (Matthew 28:19). We can assume that He intended them and us to map out our work, to have a strategic plan of attack.

You should plan your attack on two fronts—self-acceptance and the spiritual life.

Before we discuss the spiritual methods and goals of discipleship, we need to go over some of the practical aspects of the process. All too often, I've seen well-intentioned Christians fail in spiritual discipling because they've forgotten to take care of the practical side of things. As we look at these things together, think of yourself as, through the Lord, a master builder.

The most practical thing you can do for young people is to help them learn self-acceptance. Some urban young people have only a ramshackle emotional structure, patched together with a series of bad experiences over the years. As you build your relationship with them, you may want and be able to lead teens on a "memory walk" through the past. In doing so you may be able to help them to recognize (and then deal with) some of the negative things from their past that continue to plague them.

Once you've torn down that decaying structure, you can begin to build for young people a new personal dwelling, held together by positive values and love.

Your Personal Part in the Plan

One of the most effective ways to build those values into young people is to serve as a model. Let teens see you in a natural environment where you fail and succeed, work and play, laugh and cry.

In my own early Christian life, no single experience proved more valuable to me than the relationship I developed with Al Hopson, an adult who discipled me by serving as my role model. Al wanted me to see God's concern for my whole life—my physical needs, my social, mental, and emotional development. That was in addition to His obvious concern for my spiritual development. In fact, I discovered that it's easier to believe that God cares about our spiritual growth if we can also believe that He has a concern for our more apparent needs.

My discipling by Al began with nothing more complicated than trips to a local restaurant, where we would have a hamburger and a soft drink and talk about God, about His love, concern, and grace. From the very start Al shared with me the gracious workings of God in his own life. But he was low-keyed in his approach, never making me feel that he was some sort of bounty hunter for souls. Al let me know clearly that he and his God were interested in me for the long haul.

Al communicated that interest by often inviting me into his home, where we would talk for hours on end about my talents, my goals, and my career plans. At other times we'd go shopping or out to dinner together, or we might just go for a short ride in order to talk. Though he was obviously concerned about me, he wasn't so concerned that he had to protect me from the fact that he had moments of joy and fear, happiness and sadness, gratitude and anger. Al was a Christian who could accept himself and love others because of the grace of God. Through his example, I sensed God's concern for my whole person.

I am not trying to claim that anyone has to pattern his ministry on this particular format. My experience with Al is an example of the kind of relationship you should and can seek to develop with the young people you are discipling. However you do it, if you demonstrate God's care for the whole of young people's experience, you will have laid down a solid foundation on which all the rest of the process of discipling will be built.

On that base you should be able to build into these young people some solid skills. Many of them, for example, know little or nothing about how to manage money. As single teens and married young adults, they often run into major problems because they lack the discipline a budget provides. If you help them learn some of the fundamentals of budgeting, you will not only be giving them a needed skill, but you will also be training them in some key, yet often overlooked, areas of responsibility.

Young people also need to see others they respect do chores around the home. Many youth, both in the city and suburbs, never learn to look at the family as a group in which all members share responsibilities. I was amused to see the shock on the face of a young man when he heard that I mopped the floors at home. Actually, I was both amused and pleased, because I saw that young man learn something valuable about duty and discipline. He had a model to follow.

Young people also need to see positive patterns of male/female relationship. They need these examples and solid advice about dating and marriage. They desperately need to see marriages that work, and to witness in your relationship to your husband or wife the respect you have for each other, the delight you take in each other, and the permanent commitment you have made to each other.

The Spiritual Side of Discipleship

Even as you lay down this foundation of practical concern and love, you will want to construct, with and for young people, a strong disciplined growing life in Christ. That life of discipleship should begin with youth gaining the certainty that in Christ they have been transformed, no longer stumbling aimlessly in the darkness but walking in the light.

In earlier chapters we've looked at some of the implications of the fact that "If anyone is in Christ, he is a new creation; the old has gone, the new has come!" (2 Corinthians 5:17). At this point we only need to stress that this reality of a new life in Christ must serve as the bedrock of discipleship.

This new reality involves a new relationship. In spiritual terms, this means that your young people are no longer homeless orphans, but have been welcomed as sons and daughters into their Father's mansion. In practical terms, it means that young people should come, through your aid, to realize that the One who created the universe and keeps it going loves even them.

Many urban youth grow up believing that they matter to no one, and that those who do know them don't necessarily like or care for them. It's easy to see, isn't it, how young people can transfer negative feelings about the adults they do know to the God they don't know?

The apostle Paul tells us in Galatians 4:4-7 that Christians become, with Christ, heirs and sons of God. He says that when Christians grow in Christ, they increasingly realize what a change has come with salvation, a change from slavery to sonship. People freed from sin can worship a loving Father.

Throughout the process of discipleship, but especially in its early stages, you will need to show young people through your words and deeds that they need not transfer all the bad images they might have of adults to God. By grounding young people in the Word of God, by challenging and encouraging them when necessary, by showing them an example of Christlike love in your own living, and by praying, praying, praying for them, you will help immeasurably in that process by which they come to see how incredibly rich is their inheritance.

It is also crucial in ministering to young people to teach them how to handle feelings. Too often we mistake our feelings about our relationship with God for the true nature of that relationship. This is especially true of young people, who seem to feel more intensely and to trust those feelings more fully than almost any other age group does.

One way to approach the question of feelings might be to look at what it truly means to be a joint heir of God with Christ. To be one with Christ means to be one with Him not only in moments of joy but also in moments of despair; it means not only rising with Him from the grave but also going into that grave with Him.

These mysteries teach us a lesson about the inevitability and necessity of suffering for Christians. But they also contain a note of great encouragement. Anyone being discipled in the faith is going to come to a day, after conversion, when she seems to slide at the speed of light down from the mountaintop of joy into the pit of despair. And when that happens, she is likely to say, "Hey, what happened? This isn't the life of blessings and bliss they told me Jesus would bring. What's the matter?" And if the teen doesn't have a strong scriptural antibiotic for this potential virus, she may succumb to that spiritual infection and conclude that "God must not care for me, either because I am not worthy of His love or because He can't be bothered with me. And if He can't or won't love me, why should I waste my time on Him?"

I realize that may sound exaggerated, but haven't all of us heard such feelings, or even felt them ourselves when we were depressed about things in general or something in particular?

Because Christians experience low times, we cannot overemphasize the need for all of us to have a faith deep enough to deal with bad feelings. We need a faith that assures us that we are God's children and heirs even when we don't feel we are. We need to be able to say with the apostle Paul, "neither death nor life, neither angels nor demons, neither the present nor the future, nor any powers, neither height nor depth, nor anything else in all creation, will be able to separate us from the love of God that is in Christ Jesus our Lord" (Romans 8:38, 39).

You have many tools to help you in building this part of the structure of discipleship. You have Scripture, your own example, your prayer, and your ability to challenge and encourage. One specific thing you might do would be to point out the great number of times the Bible refers to our Christian life as a pilgrimage or journey. When you set out on a spiritual journey—as the ancient Israelites did when they fled Egypt in search of the promised land —you know that there will come a long, often tough, period when you will see or sense the land in the distance and yet know how far you still are from it.

That may be the largest and most important part of discipleship; learning to live with the fact that the Christian life is a journey in which the destination is not in this life. It's knowing how to keep on trying, struggling for the spiritual perfection you desire and knowing how to live in God's forgiveness when you fail repeatedly to achieve that perfection.

You will also want to disciple young people in the ways of confession. They should be taught that God's forgiveness for sin is freely available, but only for those who repent and confess their sins. "If we claim to be without sin, we deceive ourselves and the truth is not in us. If we confess our sins, he is faithful and just and will forgive our sins and purify us from all unrighteousness" (1 John 1:8, 9). Growth demands the confession of sins. You can be instrumental in this process just by making yourself available and showing that you are one who can be trusted. I always knew I could trust my friend Al, and as a result, I felt free to share many of my personal shortcomings with him. Not only did I confess my sins to God, but I also received through Al's acceptance a real sense of what it means to be forgiven for my sins and failures.

You will need to make other things part of your "building plan" as you help young people to construct a solid spiritual life—understanding the lordship of Christ, developing a solid devotional life of prayer and Scripture reading, and learning to share the joy of life in Christ. These are discussed elsewhere in this book. Once you have realized the need to map out your strategy for a personal ministry, these additional aspects of discipleship will fit naturally into the larger design of young people's growth. With a plan in hand, you will find yourself well along the way toward developing a powerful, effective, personal ministry for Christ.

LIFE RESPONSE

1. Chapter 8 centers on you and your modeling action. Therefore, these exercises relate to your own life response rather than group activities.

Take a clean sheet of paper and draw a line vertically down the center. Head the first column "Earthly Needs" and the second "Spiritual Needs." Read John 3:12. Think about these categories in relation to needs your teens have. Ask yourself how the spiritual side enlightens the earthly side. Finally, jot in each column the kinds of actions you can take to meet teens' earthly and spiritual needs.

Now put a check mark beside those actions you do take or have taken regularly. Underline those you are willing to try. Plan for the implementation of the best approaches.

2. Did you have a spiritual mentor who discipled you? If so, write that person a letter of appreciation or call him on the phone. Express your gratitude and tell him how you are now hoping to pass on that training to others.

Ask your mentor what he remembers most fondly about your relationship. Share your successes. Finally, pray together.

3. Write a letter to yourself describing what you perceive to be your strengths and weaknesses as a Christian role model for your teens. Approach this thoughtfully and prayerfully. Be honest with yourself—no one else need see the letter.

As you think about what you've written, jot notes to yourself indicating where and how you'd like to improve. These notes could become the basis of a personal plan for your youth ministry. Put the letter and notes away for a week. When you come back to them, try using what you've written as a basis of such a plan for ministry. You may wish to share your original letter with your group. Do so only if you are completely at ease revealing your feelings so openly at this time.

Chapter Nine

Learning to Lead

IT WAS HE who gave some to be apostles, some
to be prophets, some to be evangelists, and some
to be pastors and teachers, to prepare God's people for works of service, so that the body of Christ
may be built up until we all reach unity in the
faith and in the knowledge of the Son of God and
become mature, attaining to the whole measure of
the fullness of Christ.

Ephesians 4:11-13

As disciples, young people can grow and mature in
their desire to be used by God. Your responsibility is to
equip them with the tools necessary to do so. Often in
youth work we pat ourselves on the back for the numbers of young people we have won to Christ, but the
true measure of our success comes when those young
people learn to win others to Christ. Nothing is more
exciting than seeing young people share their faith with
friends or relatives who accept Christ as a result of
their witness!

Their desire to grow in Christ comes from seeing that same desire modeled in your life. Talk to them about how you were led to Christ and about some of your experiences in leading others to Christ. Tell them of your victories and defeats. Don't be afraid to let them know some of the difficulties you have encountered when telling others about Christ. They need to hear it all. If you are going to be sharing your faith with someone, invite some young people to go with you to learn what to say and do. Most important of all, introduce to them the role of prayer in sharing their faith with others. The apostle Paul spoke of making our requests known to God through prayer and supplication (Philippians 4:6). Young people who share their faith with friends at school will need to be undergirded with the power of prayer. When they make their requests known to God, their faith will be strengthened as they see Him work in their lives and the lives of others.

Two aspects of leadership can be developed as part of your youth program—learning to lead others to Christ and learning to lead the youth group. A youth minister in a city in the Midwest has a Bible study in every high school represented in his youth group. All the studies are led by young people from the youth group. The youth minister never sets foot on a high school campus, and yet through his ministry, the gospel message reaches hundreds of young people each week. The youth ministry of that church is well known throughout the city because its young people have learned to lead.

As youth workers you are the equippers. When you create an atmosphere for learning to lead, young people learn to use their gifts, which are used to build up the body of Christ and to benefit others.

Your investment in their lives will have an impact on the church now and in the future. The result now will be a healthy, vital youth group. The future result will be the next generation of church leaders!

A Model of Leadership

The example of Al Hopson in Chapter 8 touched on the importance of developing the kind of relationship with a young person that will build skills for life as well as leadership. That type of relationship is best exemplified in the friendship of Paul and Timothy.

In 1 Timothy 1:2, Paul addresses Timothy as "my true son in the faith." Urban youth are often looking for parental guidance and discipline. They often do not have it in their home or any other place in their lives, but the church can be a place where it is offered them. You may become a parental figure in the lives of several young people. I encourage you to be responsible with that privilege. Your example of Christian leadership is not going unnoticed by the young people in your group. Every word you say, every action you take, makes an indelible print on their minds.

Paul's successful ministry was a testimony to the type of leader he was, and Timothy was aware of Paul's ministry. Timothy had grown and matured in his relationship with Christ so much so that others spoke highly of him and the contribution he could make working alongside Paul. So when Paul was in Timothy's hometown of Lystra on a missionary journey (Acts 16), he asked Timothy to join him as a fellow missionary. Timothy became Paul's trusted and greatly loved companion.

Paul began equipping Timothy for leadership by allowing him to work with him as a fellow missionary. Paul referred to Timothy in his letters to churches as his right-hand man. He didn't send Timothy to do the jobs that he didn't want to do, the dirty work, but he intentionally used Timothy where he would someday be equipped to succeed Paul. Timothy became Paul's envoy to several churches. It is recorded in Ephesians that he supervised Christians and was responsible for the training of church leaders. Paul trusted Timothy to be an extension of his leadership as a true partner in the ministry.

Chuck Miller of the Barnabas Project identifies the type of leadership modeled by Paul in these four basic principles:

1. *I do it.* Timothy observed Paul as a leader of the faith while he was at home in Lystra growing and maturing in his own faith (Acts 16).

2. *I do it—you are with me.* Paul was equipping Timothy when they worked together as fellow missionaries (Philippians).

3. *You do it—I'm in the background encouraging.* Timothy practiced leadership as Paul's envoy to the churches. As Paul's ambassador he went to the church in Thessalonica to strengthen and encourage the believers (1 Thessalonians 3:2-6).

4. *You do it—I'm with you in spirit.* After Paul's imprisonment, Timothy continued to do the work that he had been equipped to do. Now Paul could not physically be there for Timothy, and yet was with him in spirit (2 Timothy).

This model for leadership will take your time as well as your resources. Please understand the type of commitment you are making to a young person when you undertake the role of Paul. You are committing to a lifestyle that is dynamic, because you yourself are growing and changing to become more like Christ. You are allowing that young person to see you up close, whether joyous or sad; you must be willing to become vulnerable to her. Your involvement in the lives of the young people can continue once they have left your youth group. Even after they have physically moved on, you can be there for them, if only in spirit. You might become a Paul in the lives of several young people, and each young person becomes a Timothy in your life!

WHO—The Model of Leadership

Timothy was not known for being the most dynamic of Paul's associates. As a matter of fact, he is historically noted as rather timid. But Paul believed that Timothy could get the job done, and Timothy did just that!

You may have some dynamic leaders in your youth group, but my experience has been that those who emerge as leaders are the ones we least expect to do so. Be sensitive to your group and learn to identify leadership beyond the facades that young people can put up.

Leadership is lived out in a variety of ways. Your sensitivity to the young people will allow them to lead in a way that affirms their gifts. Not all young people will teach a Bible study on their high school campus, and yet a young person who could not teach the study may be the one utilized by God to administrate it.

Keep in mind that you might have a John Mark in your midst. You will need to know when it is necessary to take away responsibilities if the young person isn't mature enough to be in a leadership position. As John Mark's story became one of victory, a particular young person might experience the same type of victory when you have the courage to change his path to one that will help him succeed.

HOW—The Model of Leadership

Give the young people you are discipling every opportunity possible to accompany you to places or events where they can observe your faith in action. If you are representing the church or youth group somewhere, take one or two of the young people along with you. Invite them into your home so they can see firsthand how you interact with your family. If possible, let them come to your workplace. They will learn that you have a life outside of what you do with them. It could be an opportunity for them to see that you also have people in your life that don't understand why you are a Christian and that you are also subject to persecution for the faith you have in Christ.

As you assess their growth and maturity, begin giving them leadership responsibilities. Make sure that when you give them a responsibility, you equip them to fulfill your expectations. Prepare them for their assigned tasks and give them time to plan and organize whatever you have asked them to do.

Don't put them on the spot and take the chance of embarrassing them in front of their peers. A friend of mine took a young man from his youth group with him on a speaking engagement. The youth worker was sharing about how exciting it can be to give one's personal testimony and asked the young person from his group to stand up and share his own testimony. The young person did it, but after that, he would not come back to the youth group for several months. Be respectful of them and ask them in advance if you plan on including them in planning and organizing their youth activities.

Maybe your church will let the youth group have a "Youth Sunday" once or twice a year. The first time you will want to include them in your planning and implementation of Youth Sunday. The next time let them organize the service themselves while you encourage them from the background. There will be many activities that they can learn to organize on their own.

Each young person should be able to learn to lead their non-Christian friends or family members to Christ. The first time they lead someone to Christ, they may want you to be there with them as support. There may come the day, though, one of your group members walks into your youth meeting with a huge smile on her face, just waiting for you to ask why she's so happy. Listen to her as she tells her story of winning that friend or family member to Jesus Christ. You will receive no greater joy as a youth worker than seeing your Timothy become a Paul in the lives of those she is learning to lead.

WHEN—The Model of Leadership

Some young people may be ready to lead sooner than others. As a youth worker, you will need to be involved intimately with them in order to assess when they are ready for leadership responsibilities. That type of knowledge about young people can come only if you are deeply and personally involved in their lives.

A word of caution: As one who has led them to the point where they can assume leadership, don't be the one to hold them back. This is where many youth workers allow their own egos to get in the way of a young person's growth and maturity. When a young person is ready to lead, your fear of not being needed anymore can be similar to that of an overprotective parent. Paul did everything possible to insure Timothy's success as a leader. Go and do likewise!

WHERE—The Model of Leadership

Learning to lead begins in the secure environment of the youth group. You can create a climate of love and support in which the young people will feel comfortable in practicing leadership, an environment in which success and failure can be shared. There will be both, and it is necessary for you to be there when either happens.

You can also be a source of strength to them in your willingness to confront them with their responsibilities. Your young people have a command to share their faith. That command was not given only to people over the age of twenty-one! They are also responsible to complete tasks to which they have committed themselves. Sometimes they may break commitments they have made. It will be necessary for you to prepare them to face the consequences of their decisions.

The church and youth group can be a place of shelter for them to work through the consequences of their decisions. That can make a major difference in the life of an urban young person, who so often sees mistakes as a commentary on her life. Be committed to work through that process with her. It can make a big difference in that young person's life!

Your environment should be one that encourages young people to share their success stories as well. As they share their successes with you and the others in the group, keep in mind the passage in Ephesians 4:16 as it relates to the role they play in each other's successes. The apostle Paul says, "From him the whole body, joined and held together by every supporting ligament, grows and builds itself up in love, as each part does its work."

Most of all, let them know that you are with them in their journey, now and in the future. A friend of mine gives each graduating senior in his youth group a quarter taped inside a graduation card. They can use that quarter any time or any place to call him collect, he tells them. Young people will come and go, yet they should know that the strength and shelter of their church "home" is there for them whenever they call.

LIFE RESPONSE

1. Bring posterboard, scissors, glue, and an assortment of old magazines. Ask each young person to create a collage of his own personal testimony out of pictures from the magazine. After all are finished putting together their collages, let each young person share what his means. Depending on the size of the group, you may want to break them into threes or fours.

2. Teach a series on how to share one's faith, and as a follow-up, give your young people an opportunity to do so. You may want to help them identify a person in their life that they can tell about Jesus. The process of doing that will require you to be an encourager and prayer partner as they introduce someone to Christ.

3. Invite a variety of leaders from your church and community to sit on a panel during a youth meeting. Use this opportunity to show the young people in your group that people just like themselves are in leadership positions. Encourage them to ask the panel questions about their own successes and failures as leaders.

4. Let some of the young people serve with a youth worker in planning an area of ministry. Some of the areas may be planning youth activities, service projects, curriculum for Bible studies, retreats, fund raisers, youth correspondence, etc.

Chapter Ten

Challenge to Serve

WHAT IS THE mission and purpose of the church? Many Christians think that the word "mission" refers only to sending money overseas to people who are serving God. That attitude is often used to minimize their own responsibility to fulfill the mission and purpose of the church, because someone else is being "paid" to do it.

When a young person is in a discipled relationship with Christ, she can be brought to a healthy self-image and an awareness of who God truly is. Urban young people need to learn to love themselves so they can learn to love others. You are here to help them move beyond themselves and their own needs in order to serve others. They will be most effective in doing this when you communicate the mission and purpose of the church, and the role they play in it, in a way they understand.

Mission and Purpose

From now on we regard no one from a worldly point of view. Though we once regarded Christ in this way, we do so no longer. Therefore, if anyone is in Christ, he is a new creation; the old has gone, the new has come! All this is from God, who reconciled us to himself through Christ and gave us the ministry of reconciliation: that God was reconciling the world to himself in Christ, not counting men's sins against them. And he has committed to us the message of reconciliation. We are therefore Christ's ambassadors, as though God were making his appeal through us. We implore you on Christ's behalf: Be reconciled to God.

2 Corinthians 5:16-20

The idea of starting over as a new creation is appealing to many urban young people because they often feel tremendous guilt over what has happened in their lives. The concept is sometimes hard for them to grasp, because they can't believe anyone could forgive them for what they have done or think they have done. Some of your young people may take a long time in coming to accept that someone could love them the way Jesus does. Those who have been abused seem to have the hardest time in accepting this unconditional love. They may even push you as hard as they can to see if you'll give up on them. As trying as that can be for you, let them know that you will love them and be there for them. There may be times when you don't support a decision they make in their lives, and yet over time they will need to see your consistency in how you help them deal with the issues they are facing. A young person may be confronting an unwanted pregnancy, or may be in trouble with the law. How you respond to them will model how they should respond to others.

These new creations in Christ can learn that they are

part of the mission and purpose of the church. Someone believes in them to the extent that He is asking them to be His ambassadors in the world. God desires to use them to be reconcilers on His behalf. This is where the challenge to serve comes in. As God's ambassadors, they can take the message of who God is to a lost and hurting world. Urban young people know firsthand what it feels like to be lost and hurting. Their ability to empathize with others can be a tremendous asset as they go out to serve. And the difference they make in the lives of others will make a difference in their own.

Philosophy of Mission

As you teach urban young people that they are God's ambassadors in this world, it will be important for them to develop a biblical understanding for why they are serving. Often in planning our youth ministry, we include service as just another event to keep the youth busy. We need to be intentional about service and why we are involved in it.

Many Scripture passages focus on the mission and purpose of the church. None are greater than the Commission given by Christ before He returned to God. In Mark 16:15-18, Jesus commissioned His followers to take the gospel message to all creation. One aspect of the Christian mission is to reconcile people to each other. That is done by being responsible with our commission and meeting people where they are with the gospel message. It was done for each of us, and we are to go and do the same.

This may mean to extend a cup of cold water in the name of Jesus (Mark 9:41) or to visit the fatherless and the widows (James 1:27). It means confronting people's needs and hurts in a way that barriers come down in response to God's message of love. This message of love can be brought to them by an urban young person who also has needs and hurts. When young people serve others beyond their own needs and hurts, it is a testimony to the power of the gospel message.

One urban church faced a dilemma. A family was planning to leave the church if Harry wasn't asked to leave. Harry was offensive to them. He didn't bathe very often and he said things that embarrassed them. The family felt visitors wouldn't come back if they encountered him, so they asked the elders in the church to make a decision on the matter. The elders felt pressure because the family had been long-time members and good tithers, but they didn't feel right about asking Harry to leave. The elders asked for a week to pray about the situation before they came to a decision. After a week the elders went to the family and opened their Bibles to Matthew 25:31-46, the parable of the sheep and the goats. They decided that Harry was one of "the least of these." As a result, the family left the church. The elders were disappointed, yet they were confident that they had made the right decision.

Urban young people encounter "the least of these" on a regular basis. Each of them may feel like they are one of "the least of these" themselves. You can help them look beyond their own situations and see others who are less fortunate than themselves, who are being oppressed in ways they may not understand, and yet who need what they have to give. You can challenge them to serve.

Divine Compassion

Urban young people need to be sensitized to the issues that are facing their communities as well as their world. We must show them that God is hurt by hunger, poverty, homelessness, drugs, and violence. They need to know that God's heart breaks over gangs. These issues are important to God. He feels compassion toward those who are suffering. Jesus was an extension of that compassion in this world. As they are sensitized to those issues, their hearts will break.

God is appealing to these young people to be instruments of that compassion in their communities and their world. "Therefore, as God's chosen people, holy and dearly loved, clothe yourselves with compassion, kindness, humility, gentleness and patience" (Colossians 3:12).

You can encourage them to look beyond themselves. God is much greater than their sphere of relationship, and He wants them to care about issues that are beyond their reach. He wants them to care about oppression in South Africa, civil war in Central America, and Third World poverty. God's desire is for each Christian to have a vision for the world, no matter what age. The youth ministry of your church should empower them to serve. You can begin doing this by taking action in your local community and committing to expand globally.

Challenge to Serve

Urban churches and urban youth ministries are often seen as mission endeavors. We need to be careful that we don't create a mentality in the youth group that others should be giving to them because they are from an urban community. Even if outside resources are used to supplement the ministry, these young people can learn that they have something to offer others. The widow's mite was a perfect example.

Some of what you might do in the beginning is to help them become aware of missions. You can do that through mission films, simulation experiences, guest speakers, and local field trips. Whatever you do, make it exciting!

An urban youth group visited a children's hospital in their city where most of the children were retarded or had a severe disability. If not for this hospital, the children would probably be living in an institution for the duration of their lives. The visit was a real eye-opener for the youth group, as they saw others in greater need than themselves. That particular youth group has now committed to a monthly visit to the children's hospital. The youth worker has made them mission-aware.

It's exciting when urban young people see themselves as an extension of God's compassion in their community and in their world. As these young people serve others, they can begin to feel better about who they are, even if their own personal lives are in turmoil.

The more the young people can experience missions on a personal level, the better they will understand their role in the mission and purpose of the church.

The challenge to serve can be lived out in a variety of ways. Their own church presents many opportunities for service. Young people can help with ministries to the elderly, shut-ins, and children's outreach programs. You may want them to sponsor a child monthly through a missions organization. It would be a rewarding experience for young people to invest some of their resources in the life of a child. You can take them to the local rescue mission in your city where they could serve hot meals to the homeless. Another way for them to serve would be to volunteer to pick up trash or clean up graffiti in their community.

Take them on a missions project outside their community—if possible, to a foreign country. They could experience the way other cultures live, especially one that is much different than their own.

There are tremendous opportunities for these young people to be involved in the mission and purpose of the church. You will need to be their guide in a world that will challenge them to serve. Initially you will need to seek out projects for them, but don't be surprised when they begin suggesting their own ideas for missions projects.

Involvement in missions projects will yield future benefits for these young people. They can learn to select, plan, and implement a service project. They can learn to be responsible for organizing an aspect of the youth program. Your trust in them, by allowing them this opportunity, can be affirming to their self-image.

Another benefit of missions work is that it can build tradition in the youth group. An urban youth minister in Southern California takes his young people to Mexico yearly during Easter break. Those young people in the group have come to depend on that trip every year. They say it is the highlight of their youth program. Tradition builds a sense of security in all of us and urban youth look for that in any place they can find it. The church, of all places, should be where that security is found.

Probably the most rewarding benefit of missions work happens when a young person meets Christ for the first time while involved in service to others. Many a young person has been invited by a friend on a missions trip or service project only to find Jesus waiting for him. God can use all of life's experience to draw people to Him!

Some of their endeavors will require funding, especially if the trip involves travel and project fees. There are resources that can help you with raising money (see p. 150). One fund raising idea I have seen used successfully with urban youth is to make "stock certificates" that the youth can sell to people in the church and in the community—one share equals $10.00. When your youth group returns home have them put together a "stockholders meeting" of the people who have invested in the young person's trip. At the meeting they can serve a meal taken from the culture they visited and give a slide presentation of their experience. You may even want some group members to give personal testimonies of what the trip meant to them.

The challenge to serve can seem overwhelming, especially to urban young people whose own lives need servicing. As they look at their communities and their world, the task may seem too big. The task of taking on Goliath had scared others away, but David's perspective was different. Goliath was so big that David knew he couldn't miss! These young people have so many ways they can serve as God's ambassadors, they cannot miss!

LIFE RESPONSE

1. Do a Bible study on the concept of foot washing in the New Testament. Take the group on a walk that will require them to go barefoot. The idea is to return to their place of study with dirty feet. Then close the study with a foot washing service. This can be an opportunity for the young people to learn to serve each other.

2. Plan a month of missions emphasis in which you study Paul's life as a missionary. Show a movie during the month that will sensitize the group to world missions. Bring in a guest speaker who has served as a missionary.

3. Send the young people out in twos to interview someone in the church or community from a different culture. You will want to help set up the interviews as well as prepare a list of questions for them to ask.

4. Organize a service project or missions trip. Allow plenty of time for raising funds if necessary. Make a commitment as a group to be involved in missions work and service on a consistent basis.

Chapter Eleven

Teaching Without Preaching

WE HAVE ALREADY considered a youth worker's personal modeling action and how it is linked to discipleship with individuals. Here we will look at discipleship in the context of the group in which we train young people in the ways of Jesus Christ. Let's explore together some of the things a youth group should be and some of the ways you can learn to run one.

One thing you don't want your youth group to be is a carbon copy of the church or junior church service. Not knowing any better, many of us simply pattern our meetings in the format we've known in larger groups. I cringe when I think how boring that must be for the average teenager! The last thing most of your young people need is to sit around and be preached at. If you're not careful, you may end up leading a bunch of alienated young people, all of whom belong to a group but none of whom feel a part of it.

Granted, the types of church services you are familiar with are probably as varied as the flavors of ice cream at the local supermarket. But what most of them have in common is a more structured service and authoritarian format than you will want your group to have.

By structured service I mean the way a church service tends to put the congregation in the role of spectator. Your ideal should be to avoid making your youth group meetings into a parade that young people sit and watch as it passes by. Many of your teens may not bring anything significant away from a meeting in which they have had no active part, in which they have simply sat back and listened to a message being laid on them.

By authoritarian format I'm referring to the fact that almost all our churches turn to one person (usually a man), the preacher, for the truth. The man in the pulpit, preaching from the Book, has the power. That format can have legitimacy in our worship experience, but the same model of the preacher delivering the Word from on high can have disastrous effects on a youth group. Most teenagers, especially those from urban environments, have trouble relating to authority figures and accepting what they say.

People Over Programs

You can avoid such a situation, first of all, by realizing that at all times you should keep your emphasis on people rather than programs. I recently read a survey of young people who were participating in youth groups. They were asked which was more important—the teaching they had received from their leader or the relationship they had developed with him. Overwhelmingly, the young people said the relationship had meant more than the specific content of the teaching.

For most young people, it is not the content that they carry away from the group, but the quality of the leader that they remember years later.

When you think about it, that's very much the way Jesus brought the gospel to earth. After all, God could just as easily (or actually, more easily) have sent a series of statements of truth to mankind. But instead, He sent the One who is the Way, the Truth, and the Life. Almost all early Christians were drawn to Jesus because of the quality of the man. Oh, yes, they came, as we come, to a Lord who has a great deal to teach us. But I'm sure that we would agree that the character of His person has the greatest appeal of all.

Specific techniques can work for you to emphasize people and relationships over program. Take, for example, the danger of group meetings turning into "shows" that young people sit back and watch without getting involved in. Young people need something to relax them, to break down their barriers and prepare them for discussion. Teens coming through the door are hardly ready for a discussion or a talk. They're still figuring out the social scene, who's who in the room, where their friends are, etc. This is an excellent time for icebreakers.

Icebreakers or crowd breakers get things moving right away and gain the group's attention. These fun beginning activities get teens' minds off the argument they had with their parents at the supper table or the homework that's still waiting. They also force teens to meet new friends or to do something fun together. As a result, they're more willing to listen to each other in the latter part of the meeting.

Today's youth may be taller and smarter than young people were 20 years ago, but they're still adolescents. Adolescents spend fantastic amounts of time making social discoveries and learning to relate to other people. They desperately want reassurance from the group. They want to enjoy themselves on their own as a group, without being manipulated by adults.

You need to prove yourself on a casual, fun basis. You are not brought in at the last minute to "preach" at them; you have been there all along. As a result, you are trusted. You have built rapport—"a relation marked by harmony, conformity, accord, or affinity" (Webster).

You may have doubts about the value of an ice-breaker, since it's not strictly educational. If you do, you won't be able to fake it, no matter how you try. If you subconsciously would like to disown the activity, it will bomb out. Humor is a touchy art. But if you are relaxed and willing to let yourself be goofy for a few minutes, the young people will go along with you and the icebreaker will succeed.

Non-Christian young people may think of your youth group as a religious club. They may be turned off by all sorts of negative images from their pasts. But icebreaker activities can help promote the idea that the youth group is fun, exciting, and something they should investigate.

Two types of youth may occasionally criticize you for "wasting time" on fun and games: the super-spiritual ones who are not bringing new teens with them each week, and new Christians who are suddenly interested in growing. Both need to be confronted with the question, "Why did you come to the youth group the first time?" As old-timers, they don't need the rapport building, and they've forgotten that icebreakers are for people who haven't totally accepted the group as yet.

Exercises and Atmosphere

The way we share principles in a youth group is very important. Your goal as a youth worker is to make a lasting impression on your youth group. Images, illustrations, and content are the three basic ingredients that create a lasting impression.

A friend of mine tried a unique method to talk about poverty and the great gaps separating the rich from the poor. He got to the meeting before anyone else, and as the young people walked in, he gave each one a saltine cracker. Most of them asked, "What's this for? Can I eat it?" and he responded, "I don't care. Do what you want with it." Then, for apparently no reason at all, he handed out big, frosted doughnuts to two girls as they came in. One seemed not to want it, saying something like, "I'm on a diet."

You can imagine what the other teens in the group said. "Hey, wait a minute! Why did they get the doughnuts, when we only got the saltines? That isn't fair!" So, before the class had begun, each member of it had not only gotten a vague idea of economic inequality, but had felt it in a concrete way. This exercise led nicely into a discussion about justice and the disparity between rich and poor.

I believe my friend's experience underscores my conviction that true learning of biblical principles best takes place when the group experience consists of a combination of talk, activities, and study discussions. Young people could come away from that saltine and doughnut experience and discussion saying, "Hey, I learned something there. I really felt what injustice is like, and I saw in our discussion some of the ways God must also feel about it." We all know how something we've earned often has a special meaning for us, more than something we've gotten without effort. Well, you might say that young people who participate fully in a youth group meeting earn what they learn. And the lesson they carry away from the meeting is one they will not soon forget.

Make your meetings the kind young people feel free and willing to participate in. As funny as it sounds, I remember how important it was to have good refreshments at meetings when I was a teen. In fact, more than anything else, the refreshments often got me to those gatherings, because I was so anxious to see what the lady sponsoring the group would serve. The refreshments were the bait that lured me to the meetings, and gradually I came to see that I didn't mind being "caught" by this group, where I could discuss the things of God as they related to my own real problems as a teenager.

Food is part of the environment you establish for the group. As a rule, I like to think that any environment, within moral reason, is a good environment if it draws young people and makes them feel comfortable. You need to be sensitive to what environments make your young people feel comfortable, and when you've discovered what they are, you need to work to provide them. If your group is active in sports, find a church with a gym, play basketball for an hour, and then have your meeting. If your group likes music or art, meet in a room with a stereo or with paintings or pictures on the wall, listen to music or discuss your feelings about the pictures for a while, and then move into the evening's discussion.

You also draw young people into meetings by tailoring your discussions to meet their needs. You don't have to take a poll to discover what their needs and weaknesses are. Just feel them out by talking to them and observing them. Let's say it becomes obvious that your group has a great number of people hindered by low self-esteem. You need, then, to plan your activities around talks, discussions, and projects that reinforce their sense of God's care for each of them, His initiative in coming into their lives, and His daily walk beside them.

Once you've drawn them into the group's activities, you keep them there by varying your programs as much as possible—not only from meeting to meeting, but even within individual meetings. For those who are articulate you'll want to allow time to discuss issues. For others, practical exercises will be in order. You may want them to write down their thoughts about an important spiritual or moral matter. At other times, you may want to have them role play or act out the part of a particular Bible character. Occasionally, you'll find it works nicely to bring games into your group activities. Some games may illustrate a point you have to make, while others you may use simply to provide entertainment and diversion. And at times you will no doubt find it appropriate to talk with them directly.

Even though they have problems with an authoritarian format, sometimes you will need to speak directly to the young people, to bring them a message from the Word. How can you speak directly to them without coming on as another in a long list of authority figures?

One thing you can do is to gain their trust by showing you care for each one individually. How to gain that trust has already been discussed a good deal in a previous chapter. Here I'd like to offer a few examples of how you can reach them with the Word without turning them off.

We began one recent lesson on the control of our speech (James 1:19-26; 3:7-18) by playing back some conversations recorded before the start of the meeting. As we listened to the conversations, we compared the number of put-downs we heard to the number of compliments. Another starter for the same meeting could have been to let the young people run wild about their teachers for two or three minutes and discuss the results. How do we feel when we put people down? When we compliment people? How about when we're on the receiving end?

These activities opened up an opportunity to look in the book of James at some Scripture on the control of our speech. How can blessing and cursing come out of the same mouth? Problems with our speech are a result of problems with our minds and hearts. We concluded by discussing ways of controlling our speech by spending time with God and with God's family.

Another lesson on love looked at what real love is by studying 1 Corinthians 13. Students were asked to rate themselves (5 is high, 1 is low) on different facets of real love, for example:

"Love Is Not Conceited: I don't hog the spotlight. I avoid focusing glory on myself. I strive to make others look good and never tell exaggerated stories about my accomplishments."

Not only did students learn to translate what the Scripture means into terms that describe their own behavior, but then they were directed toward related Scriptures on the subject. They were able to discover that the Scripture is not just a bunch of impressive-sounding words, but has real meaning for their everyday lives.

Small Groups

If you ask young people today what is most meaningful to them, one thing they will always tell you is being heard and understood. One way an adult can help with this need is to become involved with them in a small group.

A "small group" is a safe environment where views and values can be expressed without judgment. Within the small group, the very heart and soul of an individual person can be expressed without fear of rejection and opposition from the others. The small group is a mutual learning community in which all the participants become winners together. It's not a teaching session, but a learning and sharing time. It's a time to affirm and support one another.

Small groups can be formed when a group of people

are curious about a certain topic (family, faith) or have a particular problem in common (dating and sex, self-esteem), or if they simply want to get together and share ideas with each other. Small groups can be coed or all the same sex. They are needed when a number of group members want to meet because they have a need or interest not shared by the larger group: interest in a particular topic, a hunger for more in-depth study or fellowship, a discipleship group, or a need for follow-through care, as in the case of new Christians.

Small groups can begin in several ways—some group members might come to you requesting one, or you can approach them. Announce at a large meeting that you are going to begin a small group on some topic you think might be beneficial to group members. Or sell one student on the idea and ask him to get a few friends to join you.

The size of a small group should be from five to eight people. They should meet for 60-90 minutes once a week. The adult leader is not an authority figure, but an equal participant who brings the discussion items and activities. You should not preach or try to wrap things up in a nice neat package; you too are a learner. You are there to help the group members feel welcome and encourage them to talk about themselves. You should even try to avoid answering questions directly, but throw them back to the group to try to answer. There must not be any hidden agenda or pre-set conclusion for the group to reach. The group does not deal with a lesson; they are sharing their lives, hearts, emotions, convictions, experiences, thoughts, and ideas honestly with one another.

The results of small group interaction will benefit you as well as the group. Evangelism may take place, within the group or outside it, as Christian teens learn to share their faith with their non-Christian friends. Your young people will discuss biblical values, observe such values modeled by you and others, and learn relationship skills. Their motivation will grow. So will your own, as you become more aware of youth and their culture and develop credibility.

Rules of the group:
- Be honest or be silent. Never try to force people to share.
- Be totally confidential—sharing things outside the group is a no-no!
- Make a commitment to show up each week.
- Try to see things from the others' point of view.
- Avoid value judgments and labeling.
- Never assume that the young people know what you think.
- Don't talk too much or too little.
- Don't be afraid to become a true friend.
- Do not contest or challenge each other.
- Don't make fun or mock one another.

"The Cave-In" is an example of an exercise that can be done in a small group. Have the group sit in a circle in a darkened room around a candle (lights out except for the candle). If there are more than six to eight people, divide the group up into the appropriate number of small groups. The numbers of people in the exercise can be adjusted to meet your needs.

Read the following and answer the questions as a group.

You are with a group of friends, eight of you in all, when you pass an old abandoned building. One of you gets the bright idea to go inside and see what you can find. You crawl through a small opening between two boards. It gets darker as you move in. You notice some steps and you go down two flights to the basement. You hear a noise down a dark corridor. It sounds like someone in need of help. As you proceed to the end of the corridor, one of you sees a rat and panics. He or she runs into an old post and knocks it over. The ceiling begins to collapse. All of you are under a beam. You reach up and hold it up to keep the ceiling from falling on you. After a few minutes you realize someone must go and get help.

1. Who will you send? Take a few moments to decide.

2. Time passes by and you're getting tired. You won't be able to wait much longer. If you act now, three of you can get safely out. Who will it be? Decide as a group.

3. Now there are four of you left, and it's apparent that somebody's going to die. You've got just enough strength to let one person slip out. If the person is quick, she will make it, but the remaining three are doomed to die. Who gets to live?

4. Now come back and discuss the process of how you decided who lives and who dies.

> a. How did it feel to leave after the first decision? the second? the third?
> b. How did it feel to die?
> c. Did one person take charge and choose, or did the group decide?
> d. Who didn't want to die but was afraid to speak up and say so? Why?
> e. How do you like it when people choose your destiny?
> f. Is it right for people to judge others? If not, why do they?
> g. What can a person do to avoid judging others?
> h. What does the Bible say about this (Matthew 7:1-5)?
> i. How can you make the biblical perspective work in your life (be practical)?

The Retreat

Along with unique ways of getting scriptural content across to young people, you might wish to try another well-tested and proven technique, the retreat.

The purpose of a retreat is to draw young people closer to Christian faith and to help them appreciate the outdoor environment. I'm not sure why, but for some reason, teens often seem more receptive to the Word when they're away from their usual environment and on a retreat. It may have something to do with the fact that young people are both more vulnerable and more secure at such a time. They are more vulnerable because the props of their usual setting are knocked out from under them. Yet they're more secure, because they find themselves in the midst of people who care for them in a way many people from their regular world don't. I myself always found it easier to confess sins and admit problems at retreats.

A good retreat is a mixture of straight teaching, quiet time for solitary prayer and reflection, and a good deal of just plain fun.

Here are some thoughts or goals for your retreat:

To offer fun and adventure through the retreat experience. The retreat offers an enjoyable time to its participants. From daily activities and wilderness trips to special events and evening campfires, the retreat provides a positive recreational opportunity.

To aid in the development of an appreciation of the natural environment. In the outdoor setting, teens gain a deeper respect for God's creation.

To assist in the development of moral and spiritual values. Through the processes of modeling and programming, youth are exposed to important human values and to the Christian faith and walk.

To encourage the acquisition of new knowledge and

skills. The variety of retreat activities offers young people the opportunity to learn new information and skills.

To contribute to social growth and development. The retreat's 24-hour living situation provides the opportunity for individuals to learn to live and work with other young people their age.

To promote personal growth and maturity. The retreat program emphasizes the importance of the individual, offering opportunities to discover potential, to exercise abilities, and to receive greater insight in developing a new value system.

To lay a foundation for leadership and service. The youth will be exposed to leadership and service as they are intentionally modeled and programmed in the retreat environment.

The program for a retreat should include:
1. Activity
2. Curriculum—sample curriculum topics include
   a. Peer counseling
   b. Clarifying one's own values
   c. Bible insight
   d. Dating
   e. Personal hygiene
3. Small Group Sessions
4. Food
5. Budget
6. Rules and Discipline
7. Reentry Program—back into the urban community

I strongly suggest that you consider making the retreat a key part of your ministry, because it offers a healthy atmosphere for growth.

Bill of Rights for Christian Young People

Here are some general goals to set for your group. Think of them as a sort of "Bill of Rights" for Christian youth.

1. Young people deserve to feel that the Bible speaks directly to everyday life.

2. Young people deserve to learn they can approach the Bible for answers to all kinds of problems.

3. Young people deserve to have help in enhancing their personal relationship with God.

4. Young people deserve to be driven to seek and to know God better.

5. Young people deserve to accept and like themselves better.

6. Young people deserve to know that God cares constantly for each of the individuals He has created.

7. Young people deserve to sense the special concern of the youth worker for them.

8. Young people deserve to know that they can be used by God.

To reach such goals, you're going to have to instill certain values or qualities in the young people of your group—such values as openness, a secure identity, and love for one another. At first, such values may seem to be a means to an end—a way of helping you to fulfill, through the group, that "Bill of Rights" for teens. But the more you think about these values, the more you'll come to see them as ends in themselves. You want to have a successful group, and you probably can't have one without such qualities or values. In the long run, you will and should value most highly the qualities that make the group successful rather than the success itself.

Without openness, for example, the early Christian

church would have withered on the vine; without it your youth group becomes nothing but another of the countless cliques a teenager can belong to. You want your group to have a sound identity, for young people will find great comfort and security in the fact that they belong to something significant. One of your main efforts as group leader should be to train these young people in habits of openness and acceptance. Perhaps you should even focus entire meetings on the subject. Though this is a difficult thing to teach, you must keep striving to teach it.

Most of all, train your young people to love the Lord with all their hearts, souls, and minds, and to love their neighbors as themselves. Jesus called those the two greatest commandments, and for most of us they're also the two most difficult to fulfill. But without love, your youth group will be a nothing. To see what I mean, simply substitute the words "we" and "our youth group" for every "I" in the following famous statement by the apostle Paul:

> If I have the gift of prophecy and can fathom all mysteries and all knowledge, and if I have a faith that can move mountains, but have not love, I am nothing. If I give all I possess to the poor and surrender my body to the flames, but have not love, I gain nothing.
>
> *1 Corinthians 13:2, 3*

I'm glad to end on a note that contains both a warning and a promise. The warning is this—without a love that grows in you, and through you, all your efforts will amount to nothing in God's sight. It is not always easy to love and see the fruits of love. But in the words of John (and here's the promise):

> Now we are children of God, and what we will be has not yet been made known. But we know that when he appears, we shall be like him, for we shall see him as he is. Everyone who has this hope in him purifies himself, just as he is pure.
>
> *1 John 3:2, 3*

LIFE RESPONSE

1. Exercises that involve your young people in a way that moves them from the spectator role to participant are invaluable tools for your youth ministry. Try the following approach (for illustrative purposes, this is an introduction to the study of friendship).

Form a lunch-counter lineup using members of your group as patrons. Have the lunch-counter group get into a discussion of what it means to be a friend by having a customer try to make friends with a stranger. Patrons could talk about what makes a good friend and how they try to be friends to others.

Then choose other group members to role play various ways people go about initiating friendships; for example, a shy girl meeting an extroverted, popular girl, or a new kid in school meeting a student sitting next to him in math class. Discuss the dynamics involved in these encounters.

2. Another way to involve your teens in your group is to get them talking in response to illustrations you provide. Try these with your teens (again following the theme of friendship as an example).

a. Definition of a friend: Someone who gives of himself for you, who loves you and cares for you, who seeks your own well-being above his own, who challenges you to reach your fullest potential.

b. The reason a dog has so many friends is because he wags his tail instead of his tongue.

c. How beautiful, how grand and liberating this experience, when people learn to help each other. It is impossible to overemphasize the immense need humans have to be really listened to, to be taken seriously, to be understood (Dr. Paul Tournier).

d. Friendship is the only thing in the world concerning the usefulness of which all mankind are agreed (Cicero).

e. A friend is a gift of God; only He who made hearts can unite them.

f. The only way to have a friend is to be one (Emerson).

g. No man is an island, entire of itself; every man is a piece of the continent, a part of the main (John Donne).

3. Another more traditional way to get teens talking is the use of good discussion questions. Again, using as our example the topic of friendship, here are some questions that a youth worker could use to prompt discussion.

a. What is friendship?

b. What do you think makes friendship between two people happen?

c. Why is friendship and having friends so important?

d. How do you feel when you don't have any friends?

e. How many friends can a person have at a time?

f. What are the elements of a successful friendship?

g. What things keep us from experiencing friendship?

h. Do Christians have the potential for better friendships than non-Christians? How?

i. With whom are you spending most of your time right now? Are they building you up?

j. What are the characteristics of a fake friend? How can you tell when someone is being a phony friend to you?

How to Teach This Book

THE PURPOSE OF this section is to give you help in planning a training class for volunteers in your church. The main books are this one and the Bible. You may use these sessions just as they are or modify the sessions to meet the specific needs of your people.

The Introductory Session is designed to orient the volunteers to youth ministry and have them find others who want to participate in the training.

Training Session #1 is designed to bring the volunteers to a point of decision regarding involvement in your program.

Training Session #2 is designed to help the volunteers better understand the needs of urban youth in general and the characteristics of youth in their neighborhood.

Training Session #3 is designed to help the volunteers identify youth to minister to, anticipate obstacles, and get started.

Training Session #4 is designed to help volunteers see the importance of planning for both the youth group meeting and their own personal ministry.

Training Session #5 is designed to help volunteers see the need for equipping the youth to serve others.

After these sessions are completed, the volunteers may want to continue meeting during the same time each week to share what has happened, pray, and encourage each other. This weekly meeting time could be used for reviewing past youth group meetings and planning the meetings or retreats coming up.

Along with this weekly meeting, it would be wise to have one person who could meet with each volunteer on a one-on-one basis at regular intervals to show appreciation to them for their efforts and to help them solve special problems. Volunteers will tend to produce better personal ministries when they have a supervisor caring for them, appreciating them, and meeting with them individually and in groups.

Introductory Session
The Youth Workers Are Few, and the Harvest Is Great

As a result of this session, volunteers will understand personal youth ministry and invite other interested adults to the training sessions.

Before: Pray for the youth in your neighborhood and for caring adults in your church to reach out to them.

During: 1. Begin with an icebreaker suitable for the people you expect to attend.

2. Sit in one circle. Have each person introduce himself and tell the group something interesting that has happened to him recently.

3. With the help of the group, list on a large sheet of paper examples of "Why we need more youth ministry in our neighborhood."

4. Pray together for the youth in your church and neighborhood.

5. Explain to the group what it means to have a personal ministry with teenagers, why it is important to you, and what are the rewards of working with youth. Then give them an overview of the upcoming training sessions.

6. Allow a short time for questions and discussion.

7. On another sheet of paper, have the group compile a list of other adults who should be invited to the training sessions.

After: Invite interested adults to attend the first training session. Then prepare for Training Session #1.

Training Session #1
Counting the Cost

As a result of this session, volunteers will make a decision about their involvement as youth workers and participation in the training sessions.

Before: Read Chapters 1 and 4. Answer the following questions and write down the page number(s) where you found the information.

- Does the average teenager have a "hunger" for God?
- What are some examples of pressures that keep youth away from the church?
- How does a young person become a Christian?
- In what ways should spiritual growth relate to a young person's life?
- What should be your goal as a youth worker?
- Name some young people in the Bible who lived their adult lives by the faith taught them when they were young.
- In working with youth, do you think you are more like Solomon, Paul, or Daniel? Why?

- What are some changes you may need to make in your own life in order to become a better youth worker?
- In what ways will it be hard for you to "walk among youth" as Jesus "walked among people"?

During: 1. Begin with an icebreaker suitable to the people you expect to attend.

2. Sit in a circle. Introduce yourself and describe what you were like as a young person.

3. Discuss answers to the questions from Chapters 1 and 4.

4. Read Luke 14:28-30. Discuss what this means for those considering youth work.

5. Share your expectations and the benefits for those who want to volunteer as youth workers.

6. Close in prayer for youth in the neighborhood and for willing volunteers.

7. Set up appointments to meet this week with each participant individually.

After: Each member of the group will pray and decide, (1) "I should begin a personal ministry with young people," (2) "I should wait to become involved, but I will attend the training sessions," or (3) "I should become involved in another ministry in my church."

Training Session #2
How to Understand Young People

As a result of this session, volunteers will understand the needs of urban youth and characteristics of youth in their neighborhood.

Before: Read Chapters 2, 5, and 6. Answer the following questions and write down the page number(s) where you found the information.

- Why do urban youth often feel powerless and hopeless?
- Why will youth tend to distrust you as you try to reach out to them?
- In what ways is the local gang similar to the local church?
- In your opinion, why is the church better than a gang for young people?
- What are the two sides of discipleship mentioned in this book?
- What are some basic skills that should be included in discipleship of youth in your neighborhood?
- Why is a sense of self-worth so important?
- What are some of the resources in your church that may be tapped for youth ministry?
- What are some signals you have seen young people use to cry out for help?
- How should a youth worker prepare for youth work?
- What do you see as some of the basic needs of young people in your neighborhood?

During: 1. Begin with a time of prayer for young people in your neighborhood.

2. Discuss answers to the questions from Chapters 2, 5, and 6.

3. As a group, list some characteristics of young people in your neighborhood.

4. Share with the group some ways to find out more about your young people.

After: Talk to some young people you know this week. Ask them what kind of music they like, their favorite TV shows, and what kind of pressures they face at school and home.

Training Session #3
Disciple Builders, Inc.

As a result of this session, volunteers will begin their personal ministry and become aware of common obstacles.

Before: Read Chapters 8, 3, and 7. Answer the following questions, and write down the page number(s) where you found the information.

- How is discipleship similar to building a skyscraper?
- Why do Christians sometimes fail in discipleship?
- At what point is the process of discipleship completed?
- What are some tools for disciple making that you possess right now?
- Why do young people need an "interpreter" when coming into a church?
- Why are values more than a list of dos and don'ts?
- What are some ways you can help a young person develop a sense of worth and purpose?
- What will attract young people to your church?
- What is the most important tool you possess as a youth worker?
- In what type of atmosphere should you teach the Bible?
- What kind of Bible should you supply to your young people?
- What might keep you from coming up with devotionals for your young people like the three samples on pages 90-91?

During: 1. Share experiences from your talks with young people this past week. Pray.

2. Discuss the answers to questions from Chapters 8, 3, and 7.

3. Divide a large piece of paper into two columns. In the first column, list common problems we may have

starting a personal youth ministry. In the second column, discuss possible solutions.

4. Take time for each volunteer to identify a young person she would like to minister to. Discuss each person, so there is no overlap. Talk about ways to get to know them.

5. Emphasize the importance of encouraging each other and praying for each other at this point.

After: Begin building relationships with young people you desire to minister to. Take them out for a snack or get involved in a recreational activity with them.

Training Session #4
Improving Your Youth Group

As a result of this session, the volunteers will see the importance of planning the youth group meeting and their personal ministry.

Before: Read Chapter 11. Answer the following questions and write down the page number(s) where you found the information.

- Why is it a good idea for the focus of a youth group to be people, not programs?
- What kind of atmosphere is needed in a youth group meeting?
- How are icebreakers useful?
- Why are retreats useful?
- A youth group meeting involves icebreakers, discussions, talks, meeting new teens, and counseling. Which of these would you enjoy the most?

During: 1. Share how your first attempts at building relationships went this past week. Pray for one another's ministry and the specific young people you are reaching out to.

2. Discuss answers to the questions on Chapter 11.

3. Set goals for your church youth ministry based on needs in your community.

4. Discuss what part volunteers could play based on each individual's strengths.

5. Emphasize the importance of planning and coordinated efforts.

6. If desired, plan the next youth group meeting.

After: Have each volunteer write a plan for his own personal ministry.

Training Session #5
Making World Christians

As a result of this session, volunteers will understand the need to equip urban young people to share their faith and serve others.

Before: Read Chapters 9 and 10 in this book. Answer the following questions and write down the page number(s) where you found the information.

- Why is it important for young people to learn that they can lead and serve others?
- What are the basic principles of leadership?
- Discuss the who, how, when, and where of the model of leadership.
- What is the mission and purpose of the church?
- How can leadership and service play a vital role in the growth of your youth group?

During: 1. Share personal experiences you have each had in leading others to Christ.

2. Discuss answers to the questions on Chapters 9 and 10.

3. Share service projects that each person has participated in.

4. Discuss how your youth group is going to be equipped to lead and serve.

5. Ask for volunteers to plan a service project for the youth group.

After: Pray for your own commitment to be a world Christian, and for the commitment of the youth in your youth group. Seek ways in which you can model leadership and service to the young people in the youth group.

Resources

Resource Organizations in Urban Ministry

AMOR MINISTRIES, P.O. Box 15935, San Diego, CA 92115, (619) 463-9800. Urban resource organization. Involved in equipping churches for ministry in the urban community. Will consult with your church on how to analyze and respond to the urban community of which you are a part.

Bresee Institute, 3401 W. 3rd St., Los Angeles, CA 90020, (213) 387-2822. Offers college courses in urban ministry and internships in the city of Los Angeles. Provides a model of ministry in the urban community as it relates to seniors, youth, children, ethnics, the poor, homeless, etc.

National Institute of Youth Ministry, P.O. Box 4374, San Clemente, CA 92672. Committed to the training of youth workers and is now involved in urban youth ministry training seminars throughout the United States.

Seminary Consortium for Urban Pastoral Education (SCUPE), 30 W. Chicago Ave., Chicago, IL 60610.

Probably the most developed resource organization in the nation as it relates to urban ministry. Sponsors an urban conference every two years and is involved in ongoing urban pastoral education. Well known for program in urban education and comprehensive internships.

The Way Out Ministries, 12323 E. 224th, Hawaiian Gardens, CA 90716, (213) 429-2397. A ministry that reaches out to gangs. Strong in discipleship and building self-esteem in the inner city.

World Impact, 2001 S. Vermont, Los Angeles, CA 90070, (213) 735-1137. Serves inner cities throughout the United States. Has resources on how to minister in the inner city as well as opportunities for involvement in their project.

World Vision, U.S. Ministries Division, 919 W. Huntington Dr., Monrovia, CA 91016, (818) 357-7979. A division of World Vision, the largest relief organization in the world. Actively involved in serving the needs of the urban church through training and resource development. Involved in grants, job training, donated goods, housing, etc.

Young Life, 720 W. Monument St., Colorado Springs, CO 80904, (719) 473-4262. Committed to leading young people to Christ. Works in urban communities to reach young people with the gospel. Has a variety of resources to help you be more effective when working with urban young people.

Youth for Christ, P. O. Box 228822, Denver, CO 80222-8822, (303) 843-9000. Dedicated to working with youth. Has specialized programs for urban youth ministry. Resources available for training, camps, retreats.

Resource Books for Urban Ministry

Building Community in Youth Groups by Denny Rydberg. Group Books, 1985 (p. 109). Leads young people through games and experiences in order to develop and use commitment to each other.

Building Small Groups and *Creative Ideas for Small Groups* by John Mallison. Renewal Publications (p. 14). A two-book series focusing on how to create small groups that are an encouragement to the young people involved.

A Chance to Serve: Peer Minister's Handbook by Northeast Center for Youth Ministry and Brian Reynolds. Saint Mary's Press, 1983 (p. 28). A developed plan for equipping young people to learn to lead others.

Choices: Picking Your Way Through the Ethical Jungle by Sandy and Dale Larsen. Harold Shaw Publishers, 1983 (p. 133). A study for young people that encourages them to become responsible in making decisions. Includes workbook and discussion guide.

A Clarified Vision for Urban Mission by Harvie M. Conn. Zondervan. A realistic look at the urban community and the people who live there. The book gives vision for how the church can minister.

Danger At Your Door by Gordon McLean. Crossway Books (p. 107). Creates an awareness of our juvenile justice system and the issues it is facing. Encourages a Christian response.

Discipleship for High School Teens by Len Kageler and Daryl Dale. Christian Publications, 1984 (p. 21). A Bible study series designed to disciple teens into a mature faith in Christ.

Evangelism: Doing Justice and Preaching Grace by Harvie Conn. Zondervan, 1982. Presents evangelism and social concern as being one and the same and calls on us to be responsible.

Five Cries of Youth by Merton P. Strommen. Harper and Row, 1974 (p. 9). Identifies five greatest issues facing youth today and offers a relevant response to each. Insightful as well as realistic about how to approach issues.

Fund Raisers That Work by Margaret Hinchey, et. al. Group Books, 1988. A handbook with ways for your youth group to raise funds; a great tool for raising support for mission and service projects.

Fund Raising for Youth by Dorthy M. Ross. Meriwether Publishing, 1985. Hundreds of creative ideas to raise funds for youth ministry. This is a real "how to" book that is productive and fun.

Getting to Know the Book of the Christian by Chuck Miller. Word (p. 15). An in-depth look at the Bible as a guide for one's life. Challenges application of biblical values.

Global Issue Bible Studies series, published by InterVarsity Press:

Economic Justice by Janet Webb

Healing for Broken People by Dan Harrison

Leadership in the 21st Century by Gordon Aeschliman

Multi-Ethnicity by Isaac Canales

Spiritual Conflict by Arthur F. Glasser

Urbanization by Glandion Carney

Handling Your Hormones by Jim Burns. Harvest House, 1986 (p. 120). Straight talk on the issues that confront teens as they are getting in touch with their sexuality. Includes leader's manual, audio cassette, and student involvement manual.

Identity, Youth and Crisis by Erik H. Erikson. Norton, 1968. A look at young people's search for identity and what they confront along the way. Gives wisdom on the issue of crisis as it relates to today's youth.

Intensive Care: Counseling Teenagers in Crisis by Rich Van Pelt. Zondervan, 1988. Van Pelt deals with crisis issues that are facing urban youth. He lends his years of experience in providing insight on how to address and intervene on the teen's behalf.

Love and Sex Are Not Enough by Charles P. DeSanto. Herald Press, 1977 (p. 120). Includes activity book. Focuses on biblical values as foundation for relationships.

The Secular City by Harvey Cox. Macmillan. A scholarly approach to ministry in the city. Cox gives challenging insights to what effective ministry in the urban community should be.

Signs of the Kingdom in the Secular City: Resources for the Urban Church. Helen Ujvarosy, editor. Covenant Press, 1984. A series of essays addressing ministry in the city. Gives insights on evangelism, ethnic ministry, and a variety of topics.

Theirs Is the Kingdom: Celebrating the Gospel in Urban America by Robert D. Lupton. Harper and Row, 1989. Lupton shares profound insights into his family's 18-year experience of living life in inner-city Atlanta.

The Urban Christian by Raymond Bakke. InterVarsity Press, 1977. Shares practical insights and tools for ministry in the urban community. Discusses impact on family as well as other pertinent issues.

Urban Ministry by David Claerbaut. Zondervan, 1984. Claerbaut gives a sociological perspective to the city and relates it back to the church. Helpful insights as one ministers to the urban community.

Missions/Service Organizations

These organizations can help in your efforts to involve your youth group in missions or service projects, in or out of the urban setting.

Ambassadors in Mission
1445 Boonville Avenue
Springfield, MO 65802

Amnesty International
304 W. 58th Street
New York, NY 10019
(212) 582-4440
West Coast (213) 388-1237

AMOR MINISTRIES
P.O. Box 15935
San Diego, CA 92115

Appalachia Service Project
Asbury Center
Boone and Watauga
Johnson City, TN 37601
(615) 928-1776

Bread for the World
802 Rhode Island Ave., NE
Washington, D.C. 20008
(202) 269-0200

Christians for Urban Justice
563A Washington Street
Dorchester, MA 02124
(617) 825-6080

Food for the Hungry
Box E
7729 E. Greenway Road
Scottsdale, AZ 85252
(602) 955-8438

The Great Commission Handbook
701 Main Street
Evanston, IL 60202
(312) 328-3386

GROUP Magazine Workcamps
Box 481
Loveland, CO 80539

Habitat for Humanity
419 W. Church Street
Americus, GA 31709
(912) 924-6935

Heifer Project International
Box 808
Little Rock, AR 72203

How to Plan, Develop and Lead a
  Youth Ministry Team
Paul Borthwick
59 Worthen Rd.
Lexington, MA 02173

Intercristo
19303 Fremont Ave., North
Seattle, WA 98133
(800) 426-1342

InterVarsity Missions
233 Langdon Street
Madison, WI 53703
(608) 257-0263

Joni and Friends—A Ministry
  to Those Who Suffer
P.O. Box 3333
Agoura Hills, CA 91301
(818) 707-5664 (JONI)

Jubilee Fund
300 West Apsley
Philadelphia, PA 19144
(215) 849-0770

Mennonite Central Committee
21 South 12th St.
Akron, PA 17501
(717) 859-1151

Prison Fellowship
Box 17500
Washington, D.C. 20041-0500
(703) 478-0100

Project Partner
6432 Hendrickson Rd., Box 1054
Middletown, OH 45042
(513) 425-0938

Royal Servants
Reign Ministries
5517 Warwick Place
Minneapolis, MN 55436

Tom Skinner Associates
505 Eighth Avenue
New York, NY 10018
(212) 563-5454

Teen Missions
Box 1056
Merritt Island, FL 32952
(305) 453-0350

U.S. Center for World Mission
1605 E. Elizabeth St.
Pasadena, CA 91104
(818) 797-1111

Voice of Calvary Ministries
1655 St. Charles St.
Jackson, MS 39209
(601) 353-1635

World Relief/Refugee Service
Box WRC
Nyack, NY 10960
(914) 268-4135
(International Office)
P.O. Box WRC
Wheaton, IL 60189

World Vision
919 W. Huntington Dr.
Monrovia, CA 91016
(818) 357-7979

Youth With a Mission
Box 4600
Tyler, TX 75712
(214) 882-5591

Reading Material

Books, stories, and Bible studies to generate discussion, feelings, and thoughts about missions:

"Barrington Bunny" from *Way of the Wolf* by Martin Bell. Ballantine, 1983. An unforgettable Christmas-story-for-anytime that challenges us to use our gifts and helps us see what giving can mean.

Bringing in the Sheaves by George Grant. Wolgemuth and Hyatt, 1988. A book showing how the church can help the needy.

The Giving Tree by Shel Silverstein. Harper and Row, 1988. A story about unconditional giving.

How to Build a Youth Outreach Ministry by Bill Stearns. Focuses on how to involve young people in service.

Ideas for Social Action by Tony Campolo. Zondervan, 1985.

The Mustard Seed Conspiracy by Tom Sine. Word, 1981. A look at the future and what it holds for the Christian community.

Rich Christians in an Age of Hunger: A Biblical Study by Ron Sider. InterVarsity Press, 1984. A realistic approach to living simply in order for others to simply live.

Scandalon, Known by the Scars and *The Final Word* by Michael Card. Bible study series available from Mole End Publishing, P. O. Box 871, Franklin, TN 37065-1871.

The Tales of the Kingdom (1983) and *Tales of Resistance* (1986) by David and Karen Mains. David C. Cook. Modern Christian parables about loving, serving, sacrifice, obedience, and being "known by our Maker." (See especially "The Baker Who Loved Bread" in *The Tales of the Kingdom* for a story about the needy and what Christ would have us to do.)

Tony: Our Journey Together by Carolyn Koons. Harper and Row, 1985. A story of one boy's journey from a Mexican prison to a home of love.

The Velveteen Rabbit by Margery Williams. A story showing what it means to love and be loved.

Who Switched the Price Tags? by Tony Campolo. Word, 1987. A look at what is valuable in the kingdom of God verses what our culture has made valuable.

Periodicals

Bridges—the newsletter of World Vision, U.S. Ministries Division, 919 W. Huntington Drive, Monrovia, CA 91016, (818) 357-7979.

The Door—(formerly *The Wittenburg Door*) a Youth Specialties bimonthly publication that stimulates thinking on a variety of subjects. 1224 Greenfield Dr., El Cajon, CA 92021.

Evangelicals for Social Action—a monthly newsletter advocating Christian involvement in social issues. 712 G Street, SE, Washington, D.C. 20003.

Sojourners—An independent Christian magazine dealing with issues of nonviolence, hunger, poverty, and housing. 1321 Otis St., NE, Box 29272, Washington, D.C., 20017, (202) 636-3637.

World Christian—A bimonthly publication on world missions. P. O. Box 40010, Pasadena, CA 91104.

World Vision—a bimonthly publication on missions throughout the world. Box 0, Pasadena, CA 91109.

Youthworker—a journal for youth ministry with several issues focusing on urban youth ministry. Youth Specialities, 1224 Greenfield Dr., El Cajon, CA 92021.

Films and Videos

Casa de Amor—supplemental video to the "Casa de Amor" project. Available through AMOR MINISTRIES, P. O. Box 15935, San Diego, CA 92115, (619) 463-9800.

Compassion Project—a video supplement to the child sponsorship program of Compassion International, Box 7000, Colorado Springs, CO 80933, (800) 336-7676.

El Norte—the story of a Central American family who flees the economic and political oppression of their home country, and their life as they face the stark realities of life in the United States.

The Mission—the true story of missionary efforts by the Jesuits in the 1700s. Challenges all in the area of missions and faithfulness of the gospel.

Peace Child—Don and Carol Richardson's story of how they learned to communicate the gospel in the culture to which they had been sent.

Saving Grace—the story of a man who risks his high position in the church to meet the needs of a small Italian village, and the sacrifice one young boy makes for the sake of his village. Challenges in the area of missions and sacrifice.

The Gods Must Be Crazy—a look at cultural differences and the effect they can have when two cultures come in contact with each other.

Through Gates of Splendor—the story of missionaries who are killed by the people to whom they are sent.

Wait of the World—a movie about the impact of missions in the lives of three people. Helps youth develop an awareness of active participation in world missions. (800) 253-0413.

Simulation Games

Bafa Bafa by R. Garry Shirts—a cross-cultural simulation experience on how one culture enters another culture. Can be obtained through Simile II, P. O. Box 910, Del Mar, CA 92014 (619) 755-0272.

Handbook of Simulation Games in Social Education by Ron Stadskleu, Institute of High Research, University of Alabama.

IDEAS Library—a variety of games and role plays, such as the "Value Trading Game." Youth Specialties, 1224 Greenfield Dr., El Cajon, CA 92021.

The Luna Game—a humorous game that provides exploration of another culture and gives a lesson in cross-cultural communication. Can be obtained through World Christian, P. O. Box 40010, Pasadena, CA 91104.